BETTER DEFENSIBLE DECISIONS

Errol Wirasinghe, Ph.D.

XpertUS Decision
Support Software
Included

Copyright © 2018 – Dr. Errol Wirasinghe

All rights reserved. No part of this book may be used or reproduced in any manner whatsoever without written permission, except in the case of brief quotations embodied in critical articles or reviews.

For information contact: author@xpertus.com

http://www.xpertus.com

First Edition: Oct. 2018

Dedicated to our grandkids...

Jaiden,
Ethan,
Evan, and
Sophie

Appreciation:

My grateful thanks to Alice Bradley (www.abconsultdesign.com) for her tireless effort, and invaluable contribution, in reviewing this book.

PREFACE

A CEO may have to decide if he should compete against a rival, acquire the rival, or even co-exist with him. A mother may have to decide if she should send her son to a state college, or borrow money to send him to a more expensive private university. To the people involved, these are crucial decisions, and they need to be defensible.

It is natural to think that *judgment, experience, intuition, logic, common sense, etc.* is the way to go. In the good old days, this is how great leaders went about business! Of course, you don't hear of the catastrophic stories and the fiascoes.

(See Chapter VII, for a list of "famous" bad decisions)

I am certain many of you are convinced that your success is proof that you make good decisions.

It's the *other guy*, who needs training!

Would you have an untrained mechanic, repair your vehicle?

Would you go to a dentist who has not been trained?

Probably not! Because you know that a *trained* mechanic or dentist would do a better job, than an untrained one.

Yet, we rely on many untrained managers/leaders to make serious decisions.

A young girl, who wishes to be a model, needs to learn to walk "*elegantly*" (as models do) – even though she has been walking since her toddler days.

Decision-making is no different! With training one would do better. If you want to be at the top of your game, you need to learn to make better, defensible decisions. Yet, most of us have never considered training in *decision-making*.

A recent study (Business Objects Magazine) showed that 93% of US Managers have not had any formal training in decision-making.

During an interview, Truett Cathy, founder of the "Chick-Fil-A" restaurant chain was asked...

How did you become so successful?
>He said... *By making good decisions!*

How did you make these good decisions?
>He said... *From experience!*

How did you gain this experience?
>He said.... *By making bad decisions!*

Question:
>*Would you rather learn from your mistakes, or be trained?*

A Manager/Leader/Supervisor/CEO/Coach/Small Business Owner, etc., has to make decisions with incomplete data, inherent probabilities, limited resources, and within a specified time frame.

In any decision-making scenario, almost always there is a risk-reward trade-off. The underlying motivator is a fine balance of our desire to get the best deal vs. the need to avoid a catastrophic outcome – which will likely involve defending the decision to various stakeholders ... and, to ourselves!

Talented executives from very successful companies have made radically different decisions with the same information and in the same time frame. One does not need to look far to see authoritative claims by experts that have turned out to be totally inaccurate.

Consider the following:

- "I recommend that the U.S. Patent Office be shut down since everything that could be invented has already been invented."
  (Charles Duell, Director of the U.S. Patent Office, 1899)

- "This bomb will never go off – I speak as an expert in explosives."

  (Admiral William Leahy; U.S. Atomic Bomb Project, 1940)

Research on decision-making has, at one extreme – theoreticians focusing on mathematical techniques such as *Artificial Intelligence, Neural Networks, Robotics, Fuzzy Logic, etc.*, while at the other extreme, Neurobiologists, and Behavioral Scientists studying *the brain and human behavior.*

Unfortunately, these two groups rarely collaborate, and neither has been of much help to the typical industry professional, or the average person.

Why we have problems dealing with decisions can be attributed to the following:

1. We seek safety, and avoid risks.
2. We react to our emotions (fear), whether real or imagined, to avoid risks.
3. We learn habits and continue to make the same decision even if the circumstance has changed, and it no longer suits them.
4. Paralyzed by too many choices (7 or fewer options, is ideal).
5. We imagine a "worst-case scenario," which causes mental paralysis.
6. High-stress levels inhibit rational, higher-level thinking.
7. Seeking the "perfect decision," (which does not exist), leads to inaction.
8. Making a decision makes us responsible for our choice. If it does not work out, we have no one to blame.
9. Fear of having to defend the decision.

This book is not a complicated treatise on mathematics, or behavioral science, or philosophy; it is a practical guide to decision-making presented in lay terms – aimed at everyone.

It provides the tools, and the techniques required to make defensible, optimum, consistent, decisions in a timely manner (D.O.C.T.).

Remember....

In life, you are free to make choices!
But you are not free from the consequences of such choices!

Yes, framing the problem correctly, and modeling it, is not an easy task. You have to decide when the outcome is serious enough, to warrant modeling. If you continue to ignore the dangers of relying on common sense alone, you are subscribing to Einstein's definition of *Insanity*:

"Doing the same thing over & over, and expecting a different outcome"

Caution! Don't let your emotions hijack your behavior.

First, your feelings and senses enter the spinal cord and go through the limbic system (where emotions are developed) before reaching the frontal lobe (where rational thinking occurs). Because we experience our feelings <u>before</u> we can formulate a rational response, we often get hijacked by the collision between our feelings (intuition) and reasoning (logic). When it comes to decision-making, we humans are doomed from the beginning! That's why we need to be trained in proven tools and techniques to assist us through a decision-making process.

Some provocative questions....

- Do you really think you can get by with common sense (logic and intuition) especially, in today's world of *Big-Data*?
- Are you using "problem-solving" techniques, to make decisions?
  We stress: problem-solving is not decision-making!
- Do you *validate* your decisions before you move to the implementation phase?
- Can you defend your decisions, with supporting evidence, and arguments?
- Do you know that analytical decision-making techniques can help you survive in today's VUCA** world?

**Refer to Appendix I for a discussion of VUCA.

Table of Contents

PART I: 1
   Decision-Making Fundamentals 1
   1.1 Are We in Control of Our Decisions? 2
   1.2 Inherent Biases 8
   1.3 An Insight into Decision Making 11
   1.4 Change, Conflict, Choice… 19
   …and the Pursuit of Happiness! 19
   1.5 Irrational Human Beings! 24
   1.6 Probability 28
   1.7 Tools and Techniques 29
   1.8 Implementing Your Decision 34

Part II: 36
   Multi-Criteria Decisions 36
   2.1 Objective Setting 38
   2.2 Criteria Selection 44
   2.3 Criteria Segregation 46
   2.4 Candidate Selection 51
   2.5 Judgment Table (JT) 53

Part III: 56
   AHP and the XpertUS Software 56
   3.1 The Analytic Hierarchy Process (AHP) 56
   3.2 The XpertUS Software 59
   3.3 AHP – The Manual Process 61

> 3.4 Decision Validation 65
>
> 3.5 Cost-Benefit Analysis 68
>
> 3.6 Team Decision-Making…. 70

Part IV: **74**
> Decision Trees & D-Zone Maps 74

Part V: **77**
> The PayOff Table 77

Appendix I: **79**
> Understanding Risk: VUCA 79

Appendix II: **81**
> Famous Bad Decisions 81

Appendix III: **86**
> Answers to Problems.. 86

About XpertUS! **87**

PART I:

Decision-Making Fundamentals

*"The greatest obstacle to learning & discovery is not ignorance;
it is the illusion of knowledge"*
Lee Iacocca, President, Chrysler Corp

Like many, you probably rely on traits such as –common sense, experience, logic, intuition, judgment, etc., to make decisions. True! In the past, these would have been adequate!

But today, Information Technology (IT) has changed the playing field; we are in a world of information overload and choice overload; having to deal with *Big-Data*. There are many instances when these traits would fail you, because you did not consider uncertainties (probabilities), and human biases.

Let's start by testing your common sense.

www.xpertus.com/dq/index   (do not skip this 4-min test.)

Even though leadership is indeed top down, very often, decision-making tends to be bottom up. Because it is the stakeholders and support-staff who decide what data, scenarios, context, options, etc., are provided to the leaders for decision-making.

1.1 Are We in Control of Our Decisions?

"It was your decision!

I hold you responsible for your actions!"

This is a typical comment from a judge, a parent, a coach, a supervisor, etc. Yes! We must be held responsible for our decisions and actions. The classic dogma is:

We need to evaluate the situation, consider all options, and make decisions, understanding fully well, the consequences of our actions.

If you think you are in total control of your decisions, think again! There is a plethora of research that demonstrates how our decisions are being contaminated, if not manipulated, by the environment in which we make decisions. Below are a few examples of how this is done:

1. Subordinates limit options available to you,
2. Some modify the environment to shape your decisions; while,
3. Others actually manipulate your thought-process with well-designed techniques.

— Natural Tendency to Avoid Complexity

Dr. Dan Ariely (MIT) interviewed surgeons who had recommended hip-surgery for their patients.

One group of surgeons was told that they had forgotten to try a dose of *Ibuprofen* before opting for surgery. Another group was told that they had not tried two medications – *Ibuprofen* and *Piroxicam*.

Both groups were asked if they would reconsider their decision, before opting for surgery.

Those in the first group were happy to recall the patients, and try *Ibuprofen*. However, the surgeons in the second group now faced another dilemma – if they recall the patient, should they then try *Ibuprofen* or *Piroxicam* first. In the face of this added complexity, this group opted to proceed with surgery. Here we see how we humans gravitate to the least complex decision, rather than the optimum decision.

Even when facing decisions that have serious consequences, there are many in management who say,

"We really don't have the time to use a structured approach", and simply go with intuition.

What they meant to say was:

> *"We really don't know how to deal with information overload."*

— Paralyzed by Too Many Options

Behavioral psychologists and economists have conducted many experiments to substantiate *The Paradox of Choice*.

Though people demand more choice, as the number of available choices increases, they are frustrated by their inability to make a decision. This creates **decision paralysis**. While having choices is appealing, it can indeed be debilitating.

Consider yourself buying a pair of jeans in two different countries.

In Cabinda, a small town in Angola, the store might carry only two brands, with six sizes, and you would have to settle for a pair that is available. Now compare this with a store in New York specializing in designer jeans. The salesman asks you what your preferences are, from a host of options (See Box).

Buy the Perfect Jeans

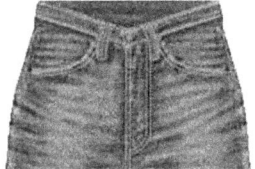

- ☐ Color
- ☐ Rise: Front & Back
- ☐ Cut: Flare/Bell/Straight
- ☐ Wash: Hard/Soft/Acid
- ☐ Button/Zipper
- ☐ Yolk/Dart
- ☐ Block: Jobber/Carrot
- ☐ Fit: Baggy/Tight
- ☐ Waist: Single/Double
- ☐ Pockets: High/Low
- ☐ Leg: Tight/Fit/Relaxed
- ☐ Whiskering
- ☐ Abrasion

Sure, if you can tell him exactly what you want, he will find the perfect pair of jeans for you. But you probably won't enjoy the experience of having to delve into so much detail.

In her famous *Jam Study*, conducted at a supermarket, Dr. Sheena Iyengar (Columbia Univ.), showed that too many options lead to **decision paralysis**; not liberation.

In a taste test, when 6 varieties of jam were displayed on a table, 30% of the customers purchased jam; however, when 24 varieties were displayed, just as many enjoyed the treat but only 3% made a purchase.

Many retailers have confirmed that by giving less choice to consumers, they were able to increase sales.

In 2009 *Wal-Mart*, the world's largest retailer, reported a 12% increase in sales, when offerings were reduced by 15%.

— *Deceived by Perceptions*

New York Plastic Surgeon Darrick Antell looked at the jawline of CEOs at a large number of Fortune 500 companies.

He was surprised to find that about 90% of the Top CEOs had a prominent chin, even though only 40% of the general population had a protruding chin.

Furthermore, the study revealed that, while only 14.2% of white American males were six-footers, nearly 58.7% of CEOs in Fortune 500 companies were white, six-footers.

It appears that if you are a white American male, over 6' tall, with a protruding chin, you have a good chance of impressing CEO selection committees. In summary, even expert selection committees fall prey to their own intuitive perceptions and associated biases.

— *Manipulated Through the Default Option*

In a study related to organ donations, scientists found an interesting pattern across many countries and cultures.

When the question was phrased as *"please check the box, if you wish to donate your organs"* – less than 20% of the people chose to donate organs. However, when the question was, *"please check, if you do not wish to donate your organs"* – almost 80% were willing donors.

This was certainly not a case of people suddenly having a change of heart. In both cases, not knowing how to respond, they simply did not check the box. By manipulating the default response, it was easy to obtain the desired outcome.

— *Manipulated by Comparisons and Ghost Offerings*

Laboratory and field experiments confirm that our decisions can be shaped by introducing "ghost" options. In a study at MIT, when pictures of two handsome men, John and Harry, were presented to a group of female students, their preferences were evenly split.

In a variation of this study, when a modified picture (using Paint-Shop) of an *ugly* Harry was included (John, Harry, and *ugly* Harry), a large majority opted for Harry. When this was repeated with an *ugly* John, a large majority opted for John.

What happened here?

When the ugly pictures were added, the decision-makers suddenly ignored the presence of John (in the first case) and Harry (in the second case), and focused only on the *pretty* and *ugly* pictures of the same person.

Dr. Dan Ariely (MIT) showed that we can be deceived by cognitive illusions. In a very revealing experiment, he confirmed the impact of a meaningless (ghost) option, by recreating the subscription offering in the *Economist Magazine*.

When three options were offered – 16%, 0%, and 84% of the participants opted for options A, B & C, respectively. Since nobody chose option B, he removed this option, and offered only options A & C, to another group.

In this second study, 68% opted for option A.

This is a clear demonstration that the *ghost* option had a marked influence on the decisions.

Ghost offerings, right-hand rule, eye-level placements, dubious discounts, price matching, etc. are used by retail stores and marketing experts to influence our decisions.

At McDonald's medium size fries and coffee are *ghost* options.

— The Influence of Temperature

Yale University's Psychology Dept. invited volunteers to participate in an experiment on the building's 4th floor. They were asked to read a packet of information about a guy named 'Joe', and indicate if they thought he had a pleasant, gracious personality; or, if he had a negative attitude to life. But the experiment was rigged with one simple prop.

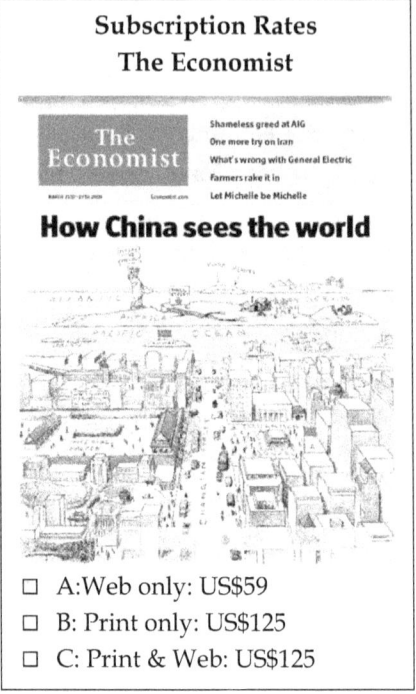

The students who arrived to take the elevator were met by a representative who asked them to hold a cup of coffee (for just a few seconds), as they rode up the elevator. Half the students were given hot coffee, and the other half received iced coffee.

Those who held the hot coffee concluded that 'Joe' had a positive attitude to life; while, those who held the iced coffee concluded he was not a nice person.

Not totally convinced, the Yale experiment was repeated under a different setting. This time they asked one group of volunteer students to hold ice packs, and the other group to hold hot packs. Subsequently, they were told they could either take a gift for themselves or a gift certificate for a friend.

Here again, those who held the ice packs selfishly picked a gift for themselves, while, the others opted to take the gift-certificate for a friend.

Advice:
> *Refrain from offering cold drinks at business meetings; and when on a date, order a hot soup instead of a cold-salad!*

— Victims of Shifting Comparisons

When you purchase a stereo system at a store, you are comparing the products on the shelves against each other.

Yet, when you listen to music in the comfort of your home, you have a different basis to evaluate the quality of the equipment you purchased. You cannot remember what was on the shelf when you purchased the equipment.

This is true with almost anything you purchase.

When buying a bottle of wine, you compare the offerings on the shelf. But, several weeks later, when consuming this wine at home while listening to some soft music, you have no earthly idea of what was on the shelf. Your mood at this moment, the company, and the ambiance has a significant influence on your views about the wine.

This is referred to as *shifting comparisons*.

When Pepsi conducted a blind *sipping test* against Coke, Pepsi turned out to be the preferred choice (even though Coke's market share was almost twice that of Pepsi).

Surprised by this new revelation, Coke went on to create the *New Coke*, which turned out to be a disaster! Coke consumers rejected the *New Coke* which tasted much like Pepsi. *New Coke* was withdrawn three months after the launch.

But why?

Because, when taking a sip, Pepsi tastes better due to the buzz from the extra sugar (in Pepsi); however, when drinking an entire can, the initial buzz fades away, and then the sugary Pepsi is not preferred.. People do not buy a soft-drink can, to take a sip!   Here again, shifting comparison led Coke astray. .

1.2 Inherent Biases

Our decisions are contaminated by many types of biases. Some of the more well-known biases are described in this section.

Introduction Bias (Priming)

Psychologist Dr. John Bargh (Yale Univ.) conducted an experiment to demonstrate how our minds can be *primed (manipulated)* to influence our decisions.

In this experiment half, the subjects were asked to read a document containing words such as *bold, rude, bother, aggressive, disturb,* etc. The other half read a document with words such as *considerate, patient, yield, polite, courteous,* etc.

After the test, they were asked to meet up with a professor – who pretended to be engaged in a long conversation with another professor.

Amazingly, 82% of those who were primed to be *polite*, waited patiently, some up to fifteen minutes, without interrupting the professor. Those who were primed to be *rude* interrupted the professor within five minutes.

We conducted a study at an Engineering company:

Several groups were invited to a meeting to decide how much to spend on security to protect a warehouse. The consultant's report indicated that the more you invest in deterrent and detection equipment, less was the probability of a theft.

> *Data: The probabilities of theft would be reduced to 15%, 10%, and 5% for investments of $200K, $350K, $500K respectively.*

For some groups, the Safety Department carefully placed pictures and citations of theft damages, statistics, and consequences of theft, along the hallway leading to the meeting room (*primed*). These groups that were primed opted for full coverage.

Both these examples confirm the view that people can be *primed* to act in a desired manner! Beware! If you are inviting a team for a meeting – an unscrupulous person could *prime* some of the attendees, before the meeting.

Recency Bias (Anchoring)

You take action because of a recent event, assuming it will continue in the future. For example, if heavy floods threaten your home, you rush to buy flood insurance. Six months later, you stop paying the premium, and the policy lapses. Your initial decision to buy insurance was influenced by a recent event.

Loss Aversion

This is a well-documented tendency – to feel losses more acutely than equivalent gains. This can lead companies to hold on to businesses they should divest.

Interest Bias

Often referred to as *silo thinking*, in which an individual or an organization defends its own interests rather than the interests of the entity.

Tribal (Social) Bias

Even when nothing is at stake, we tend to conform to the dominant views of the group we belong to, and of its leader.

In the 2016 US Presidential elections, Republicans, because of their loyalty to the party, voted for Trump, even though they opposed many of his views and values as a person.

Pattern Recognition Bias

Weather forecasters rely on pattern recognition and the same is true of insurance companies.

Sometimes such biases lead us to recognize patterns even where there are none.

Over-Confidence Bias

The following survey results illustrate what over-confidence looks like:

- 96% of male college professors think they are great teachers.
- 94% of male college graduates think they are good leaders.

We have the tendency to genuinely overestimate our skill-level when compared to others' abilities, such as:

- Being over-optimistic about the outcome of planned actions
- Overestimating the likelihood of positive events, and
- Underestimating the likelihood of negative ones.

Confirmation Bias

When people like or prefer a certain idea/concept, they end up believing it to be true. This leads one to stop gathering information when the evidence gathered so far confirms the views/biases one would like to be reaffirmed.

Generational Bias

Every generation thinks that the next generation is heading in a dangerous direction, by abandoning traditions and cultural norms.

Because of these inevitable biases, it is imperative that we employ tools and techniques that help us defend our decisions to others.

1.3 An Insight into Decision Making

In humans, *homeostasis* ensures that all organs work in harmony. A *system* seeks *homeostasis*. In the context of a corporation, a system is its *people, policies, procedures, assets, products, services, values, etc.*

> **Typical Stakeholders**
> - Problem Solvers
> - Information Providers
> - People Impacted (Pos. & Neg.)
> - Implementers
> - M.A.D. Manager
>   *(Money, Authority, Desire)*

As you will see later in this book, the need for a decision arises because of a *change*; i.e., some element(s) of the *system* experiences a change.

Any decision you make is part of a *system* and hence will require the system to adjust to the new realities when the decision is *implemented*.

As a natural consequence, implementation of the new decision is likely to disrupt the *homeostasis*, at least in the short-term.

Sometimes, a decision might provide the correct solution to address the problem; however, if the implementation is not managed properly, the solution will be rejected and the decision as a whole is then labeled as a poor one.

E.g. If the new accounting software-package would lead to the termination of some support staff, Unions might object, and the implementation might suffer.

Thus, it is vital that all *stakeholders* are involved from the very beginning. We refer to this important involvement as *holistic decision-making*.

When setting objectives, remember that most decisions are about the integrity of the *system*, and acceptance by the *stakeholders*, often driven by perception.

— Decision-Making is <u>Not</u> Problem-Solving!

What people normally refer to as *problem-solving* is:

1. *Solving the problem (finding acceptable solutions)*
2. *Making the decision (selecting which solution to implement)*
3. *Implementing the selected option/solution*

Problem-solving is unique to each problem, and its domain expert; and decision-making is unique to the person entrusted with this task. Often, problem-solvers are not necessarily the best decision-makers because they become too attached to a particular solution.

Consider this scenario:

One morning, you start your car, and drive out, only to see the *service-engine* sensor light up. Somewhat concerned, you stop by to see Jimmy, your neighborhood mechanic.

Jimmy diagnoses the problem to be a defective gear train.

You ask Jimmy what your options are, and he proposes three solutions to solve your problem: *repairing the gear train, replacing it with a new or refurbished transmission, or selling the car.*

Of course, Jimmy is not familiar with your personal circumstances such as:

- You just found a job, after being out of work for 6 months;
- You are paying for your son's college tuition;
- You just got a divorce; or,
- Your daughter needs a car for local transportation.

How can Jimmy make the decision for you? He can certainly solve the problem, and offer you options, but you must make the decision that's best for your situation.

Let us not forget that while a domain expert can solve the problem, decision-making is unique to the decision-maker, and is about human judgment.

Problem-solving is a necessary prerequisite to decision-making, but they require different techniques.

To reiterate: decision-making IS NOT problem solving.

— System I & II

Dr. Daniel Kahnemann (Nobel Prize winner), demonstrated that we humans rely on one of two *systems* to make decisions.

In *System I*, we make decisions without thinking such as:

Identifying a helicopter; that 2x2=4; which is left or right; etc.

However, when faced with difficult or complex situations, we rely on *System II*, where we expend energy to think through the problem.

The danger is we sometimes think we are using *System II*, but in reality, we gravitate to *System I*.

He further demonstrated how anchoring influences our decisions.

In this experiment, people were asked to pick a ball from a bag that had 100 balls, numbered 1-100 (unbeknown to them all the balls were numbered **10**). Then they were asked how much they would pay for a vintage bottle of champagne. The responses were $20; $7; $10 (low prices).

The next group was primed with all the balls numbered **65**.

Those primed with the high number said they would pay: $40; $45; $50; $40; $50; $80 (relatively higher prices).

Thus, the price they were willing to pay was influenced by a number on a Ping-Pong ball.

— Information Overload & Choice Overload

Think back to the days when your great-grandfather was trying to buy a camera. He would look at friends' cameras, review some glossy magazines, etc., and finally visit a store and purchase one.

Now, consider a teenager in today's world!

He would *Google* the word *camera* and be faced with a large number of reviews! He would then visit a store that has 200+ cameras!

With so much information at hand and so many options to select from, he is facing *information overload* and *choice overload (difficulties in making a defensible decision).*

Similarly, today's manager receives real-time data on *manpower, sales, budgets, cash flow, financing, inventory, supplies, transport, share prices, distribution, market saturation, future pricing, currency fluctuations, geopolitical and regulatory issues,* and more. He is faced with multi-dimensional problems and is forced to integrate massive amounts of information into the decision-making process. *Big-Data!*

Sadly, there has not been any meaningful improvement in the decision-making process itself. Managers are saddled with slow, cumbersome, and outdated decision-making tools — *someone forgot to train the decision-maker!*

Today, you can have all the information you need, and yet make a sub-optimal decision.

When conducting decision analyses, we interpret data and information based on our values and interests. Gut-feelings are themselves a function of perception, common sense, and experience. Logic and intuition are essential; however, they alone are not enough. Emotions have their place, but they need to be held in check during decision-making.

Those who rely solely on experience when making decisions should reflect on the divorce rates in the USA (2010):

- *43% of 1st Marriages failed.*
- *Now armed with some experience, they enter a 2nd Marriage; 68% of these failed.*
- *Finally, with still more experience, some married a 3rd time. These had the highest failure-rate: 74%. –*

So much for experience!

Example of Information Overload

Large companies typically have to deal with thousands of fresh graduate applications each year. No one is going to read all these resumes in great detail. They have massive amounts of information, with no process other than intuition and judgment to extract a shortlist. Hence, they resort to keywords and automate the process. Of course, no one can blame them!

The techniques presented here can help alleviate these pains.

— Informed Decisions - The Paradox

More information, better decisions? Yes! But only if we have a process to handle such information!

In the absence of a process to deal with large amounts of information, many in management prefer to take the easy way out and avoid the quest for information. Yes, in the absence of sufficient information, we can easily defend a *bad* decision. It is safer to say *"we had to make a quick decision with little information."*

But, if we have the necessary information, can we blame anyone else for a bad decision?

For a moment, let us consider a problem that many of us would have to deal with one day – that of retirement. Imagine you and your spouse – thinking of moving to another city more appropriate for retirement living.

Retirement Factors
1. Heat index
2. Cold index
3. State income tax
4. Home prices
5. Property taxes
6. Restaurants
7. Doctor's offices
8. Hospitals
9. Air pollution
10. Crime
11. Access to family

How would you go about making such a decision? No doubt you will think of a few factors. Here we see a list of criteria that you may need to consider. Suddenly this is not a *simple decision*.

To complicate matters further, look at a typical Judgment Table, with *real* data. Notice that each city has features that you like and dislike. Do you really think you can look at this table and make a defensible decision, using your common sense alone?

The more information we have about the options, the more difficult (or should I say impossible?) it is to make a decision without a structured process.

Making a decision is like weaving a tapestry.

A tapestry is a combination of design, color, and weave, all of which involve personal choices that reflect the values, interests, emotions, and resources of the designer. The final tapestry is a blend of many decisions.

Indeed, like weaving a tapestry, decision-making is an art—the art of selecting the best from the many available options, *sometimes using science*. This is where the need for a robust methodology comes in!

— **What is a Good Decision?**

Is it not true that no one, knowingly, makes a *bad decision*?

At least not at the time he makes the decision.

From the viewpoint of the decision-maker, at the time he

	Retirement City >>>	Natl. Avg	Atlanta	Raleigh	Phoenix	Jacksonv'le	Las Vegas	Oakland	El Paso
1	Heat index - AC days needed	26	52	33	29	59	20	15	69
2	Cold index - Heating days needed	37	14	25	32	10	42	29	11
3	State income tax rate% - (highest bracket)	5.2%	6.0%	8.3%	5.0%	0.0%	0.0%	9.3%	0.0%
4	Average home price [$1000.00]	$219	$227	$176	$129	$108	$157	$293	$88
5	Property taxes (per $1000 of M.V.)	25.7	39.0	11.4	15.0	18.0	67.4	13.4	6.6
6	Restaurants	2405	3681	1177	3464	1532	2312	6073	951
7	Doctor's offices and clinics	8298	7930	3668	5759	2511	3815	10515	1115
8	Medical and surgical hospitals	114	85	27	76	36	69	130	19
9	Air pollution index	100	85	83	104	78	94	88	103
10	Property crime risk	100	377	112	218	189	306	171	117
11	Student to teacher ratio (schools)	15.1	15.1	10.4	17.2	17.6	18.2	19.5	15.1

makes decisions – *all his decisions are good decisions*, even with his limited abilities. Because this is the best he can do!

The conventional view is – if months or years after we make a decision, we achieve the desired outcome – then, we can say we made a *good* decision!

The question is – at the time we make the decision, what are we striving for? The more appropriate question is: *What is the* **optimum decision?**

The optimum decision is one that seeks to make the organization or the project effective and efficient in the long term, and in the short term, consistent with its values, time frame, and available resources, and makes the stakeholders happy.

Ideally, we would like to be *effective* and *efficient* with all our decisions. Unfortunately, as we seek to be more *efficient* we are likely to become less *effective*.

Consider the U.S. Internal Revenue Service.

Operationally, it is highly *efficient* – in its ability to process millions of documents in a very short time, using minimal resources. However, it is not very *effective* in ensuring that people pay their fair share of taxes, or at nabbing those who cheat.

Likewise, a train is incredibly *efficient* – in its ability to travel 400 passenger-miles, on the equivalent of one gallon of gasoline. But it is not very *effective* in meeting the needs of a majority of the population as it cannot stop or deviate at will when compared with a car's ability.

Ironically, we have to be *effective* when making the decision and be *efficient* in its implementation.

We encourage you to consider making D.O.C.T. decisions.

- *Defensible*: to defend the decision before stakeholders
- *Optimum*: in terms of resources and impact
- *Consistent*: must arrive at the same decision, if repeated
- *Timely*: must be made in a timely manner

> While there are *known consequences* of a decision,
> there are also *unintended consequences*

In an effort to conserve energy, the population at large focuses on reducing its electricity usage; prompting power companies to increase prices.

Likewise, if people drive fewer miles, they will consume less gas. This would mean less gasoline-tax revenue which in turn, would mean the need to impose/increase taxes elsewhere to maintain roads and bridges.

These are *known consequences*.

In 1983, humans put 363,000 tons of lead into the atmosphere – 75% of it came from automobile exhaust (*National Research Council*). This was a consequence of the 1923 governmental decision to add toxic lead to gasoline (to reduce engine-knock).

The *quality* of your decision will depend on:

1. Data & Information
2. Context Information
3. Creative Options
4. Solution Technique Used
5. The decision-maker's expertise

However, the *outcome* will be determined by its *implementation*, as well:

a. Appropriate Timing
b. Adequate Resources
c. Commitment to Execution
d. Changing Circumstances

Today, this practice is banned, and we are spending billions of dollars to address the *unintended* consequences of that terrible decision.

Former Chairman of the Federal Reserve Bank, Alan Greenspan said:

> *"I can guarantee that what I am doing is the right thing, but, I don't have a handle on the consequences."*

Yes! There are *unintended consequences* that we cannot anticipate, but this should not stop us from making a decision.

> *"Do not judge the quality of a decision by the outcome –*
> *because the outcome depends on the implementation as well."*

1.4 Change, Conflict, Choice...
...and the Pursuit of Happiness!

Change is not a new phenomenon!

Change has been with us since time began.

An example of a *change* we are all familiar with is the human being. From birth, the human being undergoes continuous change, leading to old age, and finally, death.

Likewise, with each day that passes, we see changes in *technology, our awareness, our values and interests, the environment, the economy, etc.*

Even our attitudes towards *gender, religion, racial tolerance, marriage, etc.* have also undergone radical changes.

So, why this sudden surge in interest in *managing change*?

We see many references to *change* in management publications, along with many consultants teaching *change management*. It is not because change is new; it is because of the drastic *increase in the rate of change*, as a consequence of cross-fertilization and Big-Data, driven by the Information Technology revolution.

Consider the following changes:

- In the past, an employee might make a career decision once or twice in his life. But today, a young graduate will change employment several times during his professional career.
- Compared to 50 years ago, when most people lived in the same house throughout their lifetime, today most people will have moved several times.
- Today, nearly 50% of adults in the USA change spouses (or partners) at least once in their lifetime.

Change happens! Or we initiate change!

Why do we respond to change? Because we want to be *happy*!

Even our decision *not to respond to change* is driven by our desire to be happy or to seek a net positive outcome. Even when we approve the removal of a life-support system from a parent in a vegetative state it is this happiness and the greater good that guide us – even though this might be unbearably painful in the short-term.

Like the changes in seasons, some changes are inevitable –but we can make adjustments to make life more bearable. But, before we can respond to change in a meaningful way, it is imperative that we understand the *consequences* of change.

A good example of a well-orchestrated change is what happened in the automobile industry. While European manufacturers such as Mercedes Benz, BMW, and Volvo were proudly maintaining their original designs, the Japanese changed their designs every couple of years to excite the public and to entice them to trade in their older vehicles for new ones. The Europeans did not react to this until the Japanese started capturing an ever-increasing market share with their newer designs, colors, and creature comforts.

— Conflicts

Conflicts are the result of a misalignment of various sub-systems triggered by a change!

These *conflicts* lead to *problems* and/or *opportunities* (*prob-opps*) which in turn, demand *solutions*.

And when there are multiple solutions, *decisions* have to be made (See Fig.).

Thus, we see that *Change* triggers the need for *Decisions*, and we make decisions seeking *Happiness*. At the end of the day, we have an inherent yearning to be happy, which governs the way we decide.

> *Example of Prob-Opp:*
>
> A European shoe-manufacturer sent two salesmen to an African country where most folk do not wear shoes.
>
> A week later, Head-Office received an email from each salesman.
>
> One said, "Get me out of here! How can you expect me to sell shoes to folk who do not wear shoes?"
>
> The other said, "Phenomenal opportunity; untapped market. Let's build a factory!"
>
> One saw a problem; while the other saw an opportunity.

— The Pursuit of Happiness

Since what drives the decision-maker is the desire to be happy, it is imperative that we understand *"happiness."*

The language difference between *"pleasure"* and *"happiness"* is subtle, but the chemical difference is huge.

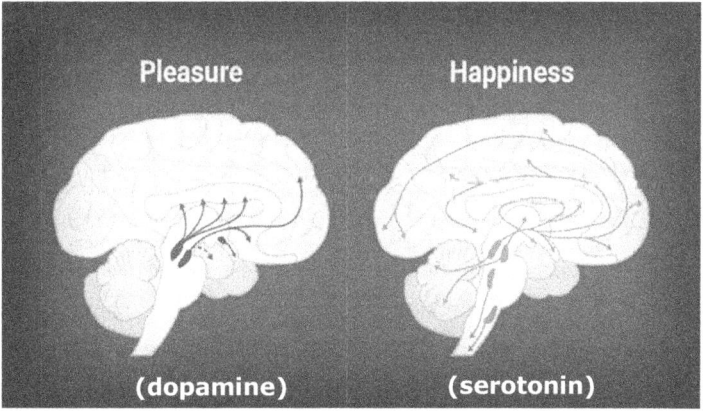

The brain's chemical dopamine, associated with pleasures (reward and motivation), is very different from serotonin, associated with true happiness and contentment.

In addition to a decision being *effective* and *efficient*, it is also necessary that the decision-maker(s) and the stakeholders are *happy* with the decision.

But happiness is an elusive target. *Happiness is a journey – not an endpoint.*

The US Declaration of Independence says,

"Life, Liberty, and the Pursuit of Happiness"

(not happiness, but the *pursuit* of happiness).

Psychologists have demonstrated that we humans are capable of synthesizing happiness, and that the experience of this *synthetic happiness* is as pleasurable as that derived from *real happiness*.

Synthetic happiness is the happiness we generate when we do not get what we desire.

E.g. A young man, who loses his long-time girlfriend and finds a new girlfriend, thinks that this new girlfriend is infinitely better than the previous one.

"Oh! That previous one, am I not glad she left me?" –

… He synthesized his happiness.

This confirms what Shakespeare noted:

"Nothing is good or bad; thinking makes it so!"

This synthesized happiness plays a vital role in the decision-making process.

People tend to overrate the degree of happiness or sorrow resulting from – winning or losing an election, gaining or losing a romantic partner, getting or not getting a promotion, passing or failing a college test, etc. These studies suggest that, but for a few exceptions (a major life trauma), if it happened over three months ago, it has very little long-term impact.

There are laboratory and field data to prove that the happiness and sorrow resulting from winning or losing is very temporary. Researcher Dan Gilbert (Harvard Univ.) studied the state of happiness of lottery winners and quadriplegics over a period of time and concluded that after about one year, both groups were equally happy – something none of us would have imagined.

When hiking alone, Aron Ralston fell into a narrow canyon. His right hand was trapped by a large boulder, and he could not free himself.

He had to make a decision: die or self-amputate his hand. He settled for long-term happiness and a better outcome. He suffered excruciating pain as he cut through raw flesh with a pocket-knife and then broke the bone with brute force. His comment, when he freed himself:

"I was ecstatic! I knew I would live".
True story! Watch the movie – 127 Hours!

Several renowned behavioral scientists/economists studied this *happiness* phenomenon. Some even attempted to identify the multitude of factors that impact *happiness* and concluded:

- *Ironically, lower expectations lead to greater happiness.*
- *The more criteria and options we have, the better will be the final decision; but, we will be unhappy with the process itself.*
- *When faced with many choices, we tend to go with the default option, or simply rely on logic and intuition.*
- *If the decision is reversible, we tend to have more negative emotions, wondering if we made the right decision.*

1.5 Irrational Human Beings!

"When dealing with people you are not dealing with creatures of logic, but creatures of emotions."

— *Dale Carnegie*

We tend to classify a decision as *good* or *bad,* depending on its outcome. Sometime in the future, a decision may appear to be an error, often due to new information, and/or poor implementation! But, does that make the original decision bad?

John Restivo, John Kogut, and Dennis Halstead were serving life sentences for the rape and murder of a teenage girl. On June 5, 2003, they were released (after 18 years), having been found innocent of the crime, based on DNA evidence. Was the original conviction a bad decision? Probably not!

Coin Toss

Let us consider another example — the toss of a coin.

I offer you $10 if it turns up heads; but for tails, you agree to give me $5. Ignoring any moral issues or financial constraints, would you play?

Probably most of you would!

I flip the coin once (but do not reveal the outcome).

Now I ask you, *"Without knowing the outcome of the first toss, would you play a second time under the same terms?"*

Probably, some would decline.

I flip the coin a second time (but do not reveal the previous outcome).

Once again I ask you, *"Without knowing the outcome of either of the previous tosses, would you play a third time under the same terms?"*

When we asked this of nearly 100 people, about 30% said they would not play a second time.

Of those who agreed to play a second time, 80% said they would not play a third time. In other words, a total of 86% of all participants (which included some senior executives) did not recognize the statistical advantage of continuing.

Though the probability of heads or tails on any individual flip is 50%, the amount you would win is double the amount you would lose; thus, the more times you play, the more money you would win.

Lesson!

> *If your original decision was based on a sound analysis of the probability of success, you should play as many times as it is offered to you.*

Ted Turner had total faith in the need for a 24-hour news channel. During the first five years, CNN had serious losses; but, Turner stuck to his original (sound) decision – *that there was a market demand for 24-hour news* – which finally paid handsome dividends.

Consider the US raid into Pakistan to kill Osama Bin Laden.

This is a great example of not letting the outcomes determine the validity of the process. President Obama was presented with several options:

1. Drone Attack,
2. Massive Destruction Bombing,
3. Surgical Bombing,
4. Joint assault with Pakistanis,
5. Helicopter raid with Navy SEALS.

He was reminded that the Navy SEALS had failed twice:

(1) In the Iran rescue attempt, and (2) in Somalia (Blackhawk Down)

Nevertheless, President Obama authorized the (successful) helicopter raid!

Message:

> *A decision based on a sound analysis is a good decision, regardless of prior outcomes.*

— Perception is Reality!

Earlier we discussed how we are often deceived by perceptions. To a large extent, our human responses are driven by how we perceive and interpret what we see, hear or feel. Now let us see how perception further impacts our decisions.

The Financial Meltdown (2008)

During the financial meltdown of 2008, the U.S. auto industry was in dire trouble. The impact on the economy, if it were to fail, would be deemed unacceptable (over 1 million jobs would be lost).

The Nov. 11 Hart poll revealed that 55% of Americans wanted the government to intervene and save the auto industry.

Then on Nov. 15, the CEOs of the Big-Three Automakers (GM, Ford, and Chrysler) flew from Detroit to Washington, in their private jets.

This perception of carefree spending angered the masses.

The CNN poll a few days later revealed that 61% of the people were against any help for the Big-Three.

This is a classic example of how perception could change our views and, ultimately, our decisions.

— Inherent Limitations

In his famous 1956 paper, *"The Magic Number Seven Plus or Minus Two,"* eminent American psychologist, George Miller said:

"The conscious mind can hold seven plus or minus two pieces of information at a time, either from internal thought or from the external world."

Sadly, most in senior management believe they can manage all the information and somehow arrive at a decision, simply relying on their own common sense and sound judgment.

Some of the inherent limitations that influence the decision-maker are:

Desires & Expectations; Attitudes; Mental Limitations; Personal Circumstances; Prior Experience; Feelings (Courage, Fear, Shame, Guilt, etc.); Religion and Faith; Comprehension (Language); Frame of Mind; Framing the Problem; Overconfidence & Ego; Knowledge; Vision and Imagination; Reasoning; Memory; Culture; etc.

— External Factors Beyond Our Control

The decision-making process is further complicated by *external* factors, which are often beyond a decision-maker's control:

Material & Physical Resources; Finance and Economics; Ideas and Technology; Military & Management Strength; Demographics; Lifestyle; Regulatory & Policy Changes; Geopolitics; Influence of Current/Recent Events; Competition; Context; Information; etc.

Exercises 1A & 1B: Perception

Write down a couple of words to describe each of these images.

1A: _____   B: _____

Refer to page 86 and compare your responses

1.6 Probability

Every decision (or prediction) we make is based on the likelihood of an event happening, and/or when an event would occur.

This likelihood (*probability*) is either:

1. a mathematical (statistical) assessment, or
2. a logical assessment (guess).

Examples of Mathematical Assessments include:

The weatherman predicting rain; insurance company determining premiums; company offering a warranty on an equipment; an army estimating the expected number of deaths in a war; service schedule of airplanes; factor of safety in engineering design; locating a retail store, or a branch office; betting, as in horse racing; lottery pricing, casino winnings, etc.

Examples of Logical Assessments (guesses) include:

Driving at high speed (safety); recruiting decisions (suitable person); public opinion on policy decisions; the CIA & FBI almost always operate on probabilities; a company negotiating with a union, estimating the likelihood of a strike; candidates seeking elected office; how will my spouse react; safety of my son/daughter; whether to purchase life insurance; gambling, etc.

Sadly, your guesses are likely to be wrong.

Furthermore, most of us do not know how to deal with multiple probabilities.

Fact: Your data is "X%" correct, and (100-X)%, wrong; always!

Since it is our happiness that has an overriding influence on our decisions, it is imperative that our decisions are defensible.

1.7 Tools and Techniques

Depending on circumstances, people make decisions in a host of ways:

— *Candidate Ranking*

In any decision-making scenario, almost always, there is a risk-reward trade-off. The underlying motivator is a fine balance of our desire to get the best deal vs. the need to avoid a catastrophic outcome. Whether you are investing money, buying a home, or accepting a job offer, it is imperative that you are cognizant of the consequences and trade-offs – before you start the ranking process.

In addition to the pros and cons of each candidate, there are other issues associated with the uncertainty of information and the decision-maker's risk-tolerance.

How we make decisions
- *Pray to Higher Powers*
- *Fortune-tellers*
- *Dictatorial Methods*
- *Egotistical Methods*
- *Delegate to Subordinates*
- *Pass the Buck*
- *Gut Feelings; Intuition*
- *Postpone*
- *Decide By Consensus*
- *Follow Established Rules*
- *Pattern Recognition*
- *Tradition/Superstition*
- *Gambling*
- *Logic*
- *Forecasting*
- *Decision Analysis*

Opportunities thrive in the realm of uncertainty. The examples shown below carry a certain degree of uncertainty, yet we have to make decisions based on our best judgment.

- Based on past performance, house prices in the city you plan to move to (to retire) will appreciate at 5% per annum. Should you buy now, or rent for a while?

- As computers become more accessible, more kids will follow computer-related courses, and there could be a surplus of computer science graduates. Should your son study computer science?

- There is the likelihood that the US Government might privatize the Social Security system; hence the stock market will soar to unprecedented levels. Should you load up on stocks now?
- When you purchase insurance, you decide on the deductible, based on how averse you are to risk and losses.
- In 2010, the average equity mutual fund (stocks only), and the balanced mutual fund (a mix of bonds and stocks), provided annualized average returns of 10.38% and 8.8%, respectively. The associated risks, as measured by a volatility index, were 21.61 and 10.28, respectively. You have to decide which one is suitable for you.

All of us have to decide how much risk we are willing to take and seek a balance between our interests and our values. Moreover, we have to defend our decisions.

— Ranking Processes

Presently, evaluators frequently use one of these six methods for ranking criteria or deciding on candidates.

1. The Distribution Technique

Where 100% is distributed among the contenders, based on logic & intuition.

2. The Scaling/Likert Technique

Here, each is assigned a number on a scale of 1-10 (1 = low preference). The assigned values are then normalized (add all the numbers, divide each by the total, then multiply by 100). Some prefer a scale of 1-5. Sometimes words such as *excellent, good,* etc., are used to represent preferences.

Imagine a dance competition on TV.

> *The judges are likely to be awed by the first performer. Not having anyone to judge against, they normally give high marks to the first candidate.*
>
> *Now, imagine your sister is scheduled to perform as the 7th candidate.*

If the 6th candidate performs well, your sister will be compared against the previous candidate and will receive lower marks.

However, if the 6th candidate falters – then your sister will look great in the eyes of the judges.

As you can see the judges simply compare a candidate against the one who performed immediately before. They cannot remember how #2 or #3 performed.

3. The Matrix Method

The matrix method is the technique used most frequently by businesses for making multi-criteria decisions. It is designed to rank the candidates being considered – be they employees, consultants, schools, products, services, or anything else.

Though it is very reliable, it is subject to biases, and even intentional manipulation.

The matrix process is as follows:

- Identify all relevant criteria;
- Assign weights to these criteria (using common sense) to represent their relative importance;
- Select an acceptable group of candidates;
- For each criterion, compare all candidates and assign points to represent their significance, and finally,
- Multiply the points by the weights to determine the rankings.

Example:

Bids were requested for a multimillion-dollar oil refinery project. The evaluation criteria were determined to be: *experience, personnel, latest technology, financial,* and *schedule* (each had sub-criteria). Weights were assigned based on common sense and experience.

Each candidate was then assigned points with respect to each of the five criteria.

The bids indicated the following:

- Bidder A (USA): Highly experienced in project management.
- Bidder B (France): Best personnel and the latest technology.
- Bidder C (Japan): Best price and financing.

A background survey indicated:

- The CFO had connections to Bidder A. He was trained by them and later worked for them as a consultant.
- The wife of the CEO was French and had connections to Bidder B. She and her husband have plans to retire soon and move to live in France.
- Several local politicians and the mayor of the town in which the refinery was to be located were partial to Bidder C since the town receives financial aid from Japan.

More DM Techniques
- Pareto Analysis
- Paired Comparison
- Grid Analysis
- PMI
- Force Field Analysis
- Six Thinking Hats
- Starbursting
- Step-ladder Technique
- Cost/Benefit Analysis
- Cash-flow Forecasting
- Decision Trees

Each person/faction pushed to assign higher weights to criteria that favored his/her preferred bidder.

- CFO argued that *experience* needed to carry 40% of the weight.
- CEO insisted that *technology and personnel* should account for at least 50% of the weight.
- Friends of Bidder C pushed for 40% for *pricing/finance*.

This is a decision-maker's worst nightmare.

Disadvantages of the matrix method include:

- *Criteria Selection:* Were all relevant criteria selected? There is no way to control unconscious subjectivity while determining criteria.

- *Criteria Weighting:* Did we err, or express a bias in the assignment of weights? Relying on personal judgment to determine weights is extremely difficult, and risky. Assigning weights can also be skewed by vested interests.

- *Group Comparison:* It is almost impossible to evaluate five or six candidates as a group with regard to multiple criteria and accurately determine relative superiority.

4. The Decision-Tree (DT) Technique*

The DT Technique can be used only when the decision is based on a single criterion (e.g. *Price, Value, Votes,* etc.). Here it is imperative that you have quantifiable probabilities, even if they are guesses.

5. The Analytic Hierarchy Process (AHP)*

The AHP technique is highly recommended for multi-criteria decision-making.

6. The PayOff (Decision) Table*

In the face of uncertainties, the PayOff Table is extremely useful.

---

* Techniques 4, 5, and 6 are discussed in detail in the ensuing chapters.

1.8 Implementing Your Decision

Why are most Americans overweight? Have they not been told of the need to keep their weight under control? An overweight person is prone to high blood pressure, diabetes, cardiac problems, problems with joints, etc. Yes, we have all been well-schooled on the problems of obesity. At one time or another, all of us have made attempts to get our weight under control. Yet many of us fail.

We do well when it comes to taking care of our vehicles and other possessions, but neglect our health. The problem is not in the decision-making but in its implementation!

The successful outcome depends on the *quality* of the decision <u>and</u> its *implementation*. The latter itself is dependent on *Resources, Timing, Commitment and Persistence, and Changing Circumstances* explained below.

— *Resources*

Even an excellent decision has no chance of success unless we dedicate adequate resource for its implementation. Where resources are concerned, pay particular attention to the 6 Ms.

> **Resources (the 6Ms)**
> 1. Manpower
> 2. Materials
> 3. Money
> 4. Methods
> 5. Machinery/Tools
> 6. Minutes

— *Timing*

Think for a moment how natural, and important, *timing* is.

If you decide to approach your supervisor for a favor, you would no doubt wait for a moment when he is not under pressure; when he is in a good mood. Yet, when it comes to implementing your well-thought-out decision, you completely forget how critical timing is. You become emotionally attached to your decision and try to execute it immediately.

When soldiers are deployed on enemy beaches, military strategists seek the best approach, paying attention to the geography and the terrain. Then they might wait till nightfall, avoiding a full moon and seeking the appropriate tide before they move. *This is timing!*

— Commitment & Persistence

The path between today's dream and tomorrow's reality is often long and arduous. You might encounter moments of difficulty and frustration. You must find ways to circumvent them. If you want to succeed, you need to proceed with tenacious persistence and a fervent commitment. Without persistence, you are less likely to achieve your goals and objectives.

— Changing Circumstances

When we refer to *changing circumstance* we mean – the presence of new information that impacts our venture.

Here, we use the term *risk* when referring to external and environmental changes, whether known or unknown. It is important to recognize that sometimes we might know the type or the source of the risk, but not its impact on our venture.

Still wondering if we need help....?

Consider a soldier shooting at a target. We position the target some distance away, such that he achieves a 50% hit-rate.

Now let us give him a *scope* to mount on his gun (similar to what snipers use). Undoubtedly, his hit-rate would go up significantly, say to 70%.

Now we give him a *tripod* as well, on which to steady his gun. As one would expect, his hit-rate would go up still further, say to 90%.

Note that we did not change the soldier; we simply gave him the tools to improve his performance.

Similarly, we cannot remove you from the decision-making process; it has to be *your* decision! But we can give you the tools and the training to help you make better, consistent, defensible decisions.

PART II: 2

Multi-Criteria Decisions

"It ain't what you don't know that gets you into trouble;
it's what you know for sure that just ain't so."

Mark Twain

Now that you understand the basics of decision-making, and appreciate the need for a reliable process, you are ready to apply the seven steps to make optimal decisions.

Consider a golfer hitting a ball.

He studies factors such as the terrain, distance, humidity, wind, etc., and then determines the desired trajectory. He knows which iron he should use, and where the ball should end up. However, at the time he strikes the ball, his only hope is the techniques he had developed, and practiced every day! He relies on a process.

> **The Seven-Step Decision-Making Process**
> 1. Clearly define your objective
> 2. Identify all relevant criteria
> 3. Extract obligatory criteria
> 4. Creatively identify all available candidates (options) that meet all prerequisites (problem-solving)
> 5. Gather information on candidates (Judgment table)
> 6. Assign weights to the obligatory criteria
> 7. Rank candidates

Just like where the golf-ball would land, the final outcome of our decision would be known sometime later; and in some cases many years later. At the time we make a decision, our only hope is a reliable process.

I assure you that, irrespective of the amount of time and resources you dedicate to information gathering – the techniques presented in this book will guide you to a decision that will be better than one based on plain logic and intuition (that best represents your values, interests, time frame, and resources).

Not every decision can/should be simulated or modeled.

- *Strategic* decisions cannot be modeled easily.
- *Operational* decisions can be dealt with, through experience, judgment, intuition, etc.
- *Emergency* decisions must be quick, and decisive.
- *Resource Investment* decisions (of time, money, effort, etc.,) should ideally be modeled; especially if the consequences are serious.

In this day and age of big-data, simulation provides non-intuitive insights and confidence through clarity.

2.1 Objective Setting

*"Most high officials learn how to make decisions,
but not what decisions to make."*
- Henry Kissinger, former US Secretary of State

Very often, we think we have a good idea of the problem. But what we see are the symptoms, not the root causes. Understanding the problem does not mean you understand the required solution – a hastily formulated objective might lead to more problems. Before we rush to solve a problem, we need to develop an unambiguous objective.

Furthermore, it is difficult to generate a list of criteria if the objective is vague. A good example of vagueness prevails in the gas industry, where the term *capacity* has many definitions. There is *design capacity, certified capacity, firm capacity, operational capacity, seasonal capacity*, etc., each with a very specific, legal definition. Thus, it is not enough for management to say that we need to *increase capacity*.

How can you increase or decrease something if you don't know what is expected of you? It is imperative that we are clear about our primary objective.

Similarly, if someone were to ask me: "What is the *value* of your house;" there are many valid responses.

- There is an *emotional value*: I would not move unless someone offered me a ridiculously high price. It is our ancestral home and has a sentimental value; besides, I like it.

- The *market value*: what someone would pay if I put it up for sale without any rush to sell it.

- The *recovery value*: determined by my cost, potential relocation expense, etc., if I have to sell and yet do not wish to lose on the deal.

- It has a *fire-sale value*: if I have to move in a hurry, or if I have an urgent need for cash.

- The *appraised value*: which the bank would use to determine the mortgage loan.
- There is the *taxable value*: the amount at which the house is appraised by the local authorities for taxation purposes.
- Finally, there is the *replacement value*: which is set by insurance companies.

Similarly, if you define your problem as *how to increase the energy supply by the year 2020,* you will overlook the problem of *how to decrease energy consumption.*

When Ronald Reagan was elected president, the U.S. foreign policy was based on *fighting communism*. However, once Reagan took office, he introduced a new policy: *spreading democracy*. There was a marked difference—under *fighting communism*, the U.S. was supporting and financing dictators and propping up brutal regimes, in exchange for their cooperation in the battle against communism. This would not be the case under the revised foreign policy.

In the late 90s, strategists at Burger King (B-K) noticed the trend toward a healthy lifestyle as indicated by:

- An increase in the sales of vitamins,
- Opening of whole-food stores,
- Growth in the fitness industry, etc.

Thinking that society was becoming more health-conscious, B-K developed a "flame-broiled" Chicken Burger and spent millions of dollars to launch it. *Alas, it was a dismal failure! Why?*

Strategists at B-K started with a wrong premise—they assumed that people go to a fast-food outlet for a healthy meal. This led to the erroneous objective of *adding a healthy meal to the menu*. Surveys have shown the only reason people go to a fast-food restaurant is, for a *quick, cheap, palatable* meal to satisfy their hunger. B-K started with a bad assumption!

And it was not only B-K who got it wrong! There were others who rode this wagon—going the wrong way!

- McDonald's abandoned the *McLean* burger.
- Pizza Hut shelved the *low-fat* pizza.
- Kentucky Fried Chicken abandoned the *skinless* variety.

The U.S. Department of Agriculture saw an impending shortage of food as a result of the rapidly increasing population, and the loss of agriculture lands (these were being converted to residential properties). They commissioned a study to produce a *high-yielding corn plant* (objective). After eighteen months and millions of dollars in expenditure, they came up with a *super* plant.

While this plant was indeed capable of producing more corn, it could not thrive in close proximity to other plants; it needed more space; thus fewer plants per acre, and less yield per acre.

Finally, they initiated a new project, this time with the "correct" objective: *"to maximize yield per acre; not yield per plant."*

During the Vietnam War, the US Army did a great job training their soldiers to have superb *marksmanship* skills. Yet, surveys revealed that only 25% of soldiers actually fired at the enemy!

Subsequently, a new objective was established – to provide training in *killing* skills. Six months later, the Army revealed that 100% of the soldiers had fired at the enemy.

Many people/businesses do not reveal or understand their real objective.

- For most politicians, the primary objective is to get *(re)elected*. Serving the electorate is a tactical move.
- An auto repair shop is in the business of providing *assurance & reliability*; fixing cars is a tactical activity.
- A stockbroker is in the business of *gathering and retaining assets*. Preservation of capital, higher returns, consistent growth, etc., are tactical activities directed at achieving this objective.

Successful objective-setting deals with framing the problem. Wherever possible make sure your objective meets S.M.A.R.T.Y.

Most people have used "S.M.A.R.T." – but we encourage you to include the "*why*" (Y), as part of your objective.

— Secondary Objectives

Sometimes, when framing the problem, we have to deal with multiple objectives or secondary objectives.

On the Middle-East problem, President George W. Bush had to appear to be impartial; but he also had to appease the Republican voters. A Gallup poll indicated that 66% of the Republican voters were sympathetic to the Israelis, while only 8% supported the Palestinians. Naturally, Republican politicians insisted that "voter-acceptance" become one of the criteria in any solution.

S.M.A.R.T.Y. Objective

- Must be "**S**pecific" & unambiguous
- Progress must be "**M**easurable"
- It must be realistically "**A**ttainable"
- Must be "**R**elevant" to the larger objective
- Must be "**T**ime" bound
- Always ask "Why" (**Y**)

The Vital "Why" Questions

1. *Why* do it?
2. *Why* do it now?
3. *Why* was it not done before?
4. *Why* we should NOT do it?

This meant the President had a secondary objective – *electability*. This became a dominant criterion which had little to do with the Middle East crisis, but everything to do with the Republicans remaining in power.

If you still have doubts, consider this...

In 1968, US President Lyndon Johnson was very close to a peace deal in Vietnam. However, behind the scenes, then-presidential candidate Richard Nixon was speaking with North and South Vietnamese trying to derail the peace talks in Paris because peace in Vietnam would have guaranteed the election of Nixon's rival Hubert Humphrey. Here again, electability was a criterion.

[Source: "X" Files on Nixon's Treason, declassified recently]

— Surrogate Objectives

Earlier we stressed the need to follow S.M.A.R.T.Y. when developing objectives. However, sometimes *measuring* of progress can be difficult to pinpoint.

Consider the issue of cardiac problems.

It is well known that most cardiac problems are related to the narrowing of arteries. Thus, the objective should be to reduce plaque build-up. However, there is no way to measure plaque without surgical intervention. Therefore, we have to settle for a "surrogate objective" – a different endpoint that we can measure – *to measure the cholesterol level before and after treatment.*

— The Domain Boundary of the Objective

The objective must consider the domain or the limiting boundaries. Sometimes the localized domain boundary is a result of ignorance, but in many cases, it is based on greed.

E.g. Imagine a farm located near a river. The farmer is considering investing in breeding pigs. The feasibility study shows the project to be financially attractive. However, one of the assumptions was to dispose of the waste into a nearby river. The farmer is not concerned with the damage to the quality of water, harmful health effects on the populations downstream, etc. He decides that his control domain is the "farm boundaries."

Unfortunately, this is a very short-sighted view. Sooner or later regulatory authorities would ban this practice, and might even require the farmer to pay for the subsequent clean-up effort, which might even bankrupt the farmer.

The same is true of the Coal Industry, and the Nuclear Power Industry. In the past, they considered waste disposal, and environmental remediation, outside of their domain boundary.

— The Time Horizon

Consider the impact of your decision over time, especially since we are seeking to be happy over this time period.

— Business Objectives

As a minimum, all business objectives should address:

Price; Terms; Deliverables; Warranties, and Remedies!

Additionally, always have an *"exit clause"*!

— OPSAMINMAX

Be clear if the objective is to *optimize, satisfy, minimize* losses, or *maximize* gains.

2.2 Criteria Selection

All decisions are driven by a set of factors (criteria), which must also include the decision-maker's resources, time frame, values, interests, etc.

Let us say you are a member of the Olympic Committee responsible for finding the venue for the next Olympic competition. Factors you might consider are:

Political climate; safety of participants; international travel facilities; weather; hotel accommodation; local transport; broadcasting facilities; quality of facilities; communications; scalability; reliability of utilities; etc.

A parallel situation might be if your company is planning to open a branch office in another city.

Criteria selection is not an easy task; at times it is like groping in the dark. Even experienced professionals miss applicable criteria, only to be surprised when a competitor steals a deal. At such times you need people with diverse experience to come to your rescue.

The best approach to criteria selection is to start with as many as you can think of, and then use an algorithmic technique, to extract the most relevant ones.

Selecting the most relevant criteria is vital to making the optimum decision. Hopefully, by now, you appreciate the need to spend time, and resources, to identify all relevant criteria. If you miss an important criterion – you might reach a sub-optimal decision!

Message: *Make sure you have a good handle on your criteria!*

Exercise 2: Oil Price Crisis

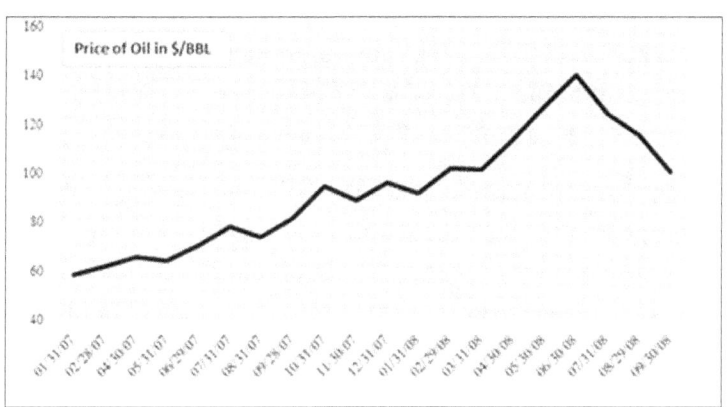

Recall the sudden surge in the price of crude oil in July 2008 (see fig.) Write down the factors that you think caused this price surge.

Now, refer to page 86 and see if you identified one very significant criterion.

2.3 Criteria Segregation

Now that you have identified all the relevant criteria, what next?

Note that all criteria do not have the same significance or importance. If you ask a homebuyer to rate the *need to be close to work* vs. *the need to live in a safe neighborhood*, they are not likely to be of equal importance.

Surveys have shown that most people start with the assumption that all criteria are of equal value, and then shift their values from one to the next. Your final decision will depend heavily on the relative importance you place on your criteria. The weight assigned to each should truly represent your desires. Applying a disciplined/structured approach will serve you well.

— Criteria: More is not better!

A very common fallacy is that the more criteria you include, the better will be the decision. An inexperienced manager is likely to include every conceivable criterion in the evaluation process. Our studies of selection processes used in *dating services, real estate, employee recruiting, bid evaluations, etc.,* demonstrated quite convincingly that using a large number of criteria is counter-productive, as it tends to dilute the impact of the more significant criteria.

This is best understood with a simple example:

Imagine that you are buying a house and you decide on ten criteria, and you simply assign equal weights to each of them (10% to each).

Your spouse then insists on adding five criteria of her own. Now, you have to redistribute your weights (assuming equal distribution again). This time each criterion would have 6.67%. Your criteria no longer have the same (original) significance. Increasing the number of criteria might dilute the significance/influence of more important criteria.

Obviously, all criteria do not have the same significance. Start by selecting an adequate number of criteria, but try not to exceed twenty. Now segregate the criteria into the following:

- Prerequisites (required for candidate selection)
- Obligatory (for ranking candidates; do not exceed 12 criteria; preferably around 8)
- Desirable (Nice-to-have features)

— *Prerequisites*

Prerequisites are criteria. Once we have a list of candidates, we need to validate them. A candidate that does not meet the prerequisites should be rejected.

Consider the minimum vehicle emission requirements for automobiles, set by the Government. Any used car dealer considering importing vehicles would set these as prerequisites. Candidate vehicles under consideration either do or do not meet these prerequisites.

Imagine you are looking for a project manager for a client in Saudi Arabia. The client specifies that the person should be non-Jewish; this is a prerequisite, specified *a priori*. The client might even insist that the person is a male, and of the Islamic faith.

These in/out guidelines must be well-defined and handled with care. Since you would reject any candidate that does not meet the prerequisites, it is imperative that you pay close attention to the assumptions governing prerequisites; otherwise, you might exclude a perfectly suitable candidate.

Prerequisite criteria and *Desirable* criteria are not considered in the candidate ranking process.

— *Extracting Obligatory Criteria*

After we remove the prerequisites we need to extract obligatory criteria. These are the criteria that would be used to rank candidates. Here are the steps:

1. Use the Manual Pairwise technique or the XpertUS software to assign criteria weights. Do not consider candidates at this time.

2. Now sort them from top to bottom (criterion with the highest weight at the top).

3. Add the weights starting from the top. When the total reaches about 85%, review the weights assigned to the remaining criteria. You will notice that the weights attached to these criteria are quite insignificant. These leftover criteria are in fact the *desirable* criteria. (Desirable criteria are not considered in the ranking process)

Generally, you should aim for about 8-12 *obligatory* criteria.

Note that the 85% cutoff limit is not cast in stone. Choose a cutoff limit that you think is suitable to remove criteria that have a low significance.

Wherever possible use the AHP Pairwise technique (Analytic Hierarchy Process, discussed in Part III) to select the obligatory (evaluation) criteria. Unless you are an experienced decision-maker, I recommend that you do not include candidates at this time.

— "Bogey" Criteria

It is imperative that you pay attention to criteria that might be detrimental to your objective.

1. *Linkage Effects*

Will the final decision have an impact in other areas?

E.g. The United Nations giving some concession to one Nation should be aware of the implications when dealing with other Nations.

2. *Exit Implications*

Two warehouses (candidate solutions) might seem equally acceptable. However, if there is a need to prematurely exit, what are the consequences?

3. *Negative Consequences*

Most evaluations tend to focus on the benefits. However, sometimes it may be necessary to focus on the least harmful or damaging option.

— Top-Skewed Scenarios

During your evaluation, watch for a condition we refer to as *top-skewed*.

Example:

A purchasing manager buying automobiles for his fleet of vehicles might assign a 30% weight to the *reliability* criterion.

It turns out that all the candidate vehicles are highly reliable, and there is not much that separates them. The heavyweight assigned for *reliability* dwarfs the impact of the other criteria. We call this a *top-skewed* scenario.

In such a case *reliability* should be a prerequisite. After candidates are selected and pre-qualified, remove this criterion from the evaluation.

— Assumptions

When you have to make a decision you start with some assumptions. These translate into criteria, which in turn are the prerequisites, etc. Often, it is advisable to see how sensitive your decision is to a particular assumption.

For many years, battles against terrorists and assassins were based on the assumption that the perpetrators would want to preserve their own lives. However, with the advent of the cult of *suicide-bombers*, law enforcement agencies have been forced to review all their security measures and procedures. Likewise, airline security systems have been thrown into total disarray. *Always challenge your assumptions!*

Often, additional criteria surface during the information-gathering phase. As you think more about a problem and start gathering information, you will often detect other relevant criteria. Add these new criteria to your original list and repeat this criteria segregation process.

Always try to state your criteria in positive terms. This will lead to less confusion and better judgment. Also, try to be specific; *room temperature* does not indicate your preference; warm or cold is more accurate, but temperature in degrees is even more accurate!

Consider the following true story:

A U.S. company manufacturing desalination plants wanted to hire a marketing manager to market their proprietary desalination plants in Saudi Arabia. Their human resources department (HR) identified a multitude of criteria. They interviewed six candidates and finally selected Randy Levy. All credit to the HR folk, who recognized that the position had to be filled with a male since the Arabs do not particularly like women in negotiating roles. The company made an offer, Randy accepted, and immediately started learning the basics of the desalination trade.

However, it was only when they applied for Randy's visa, did they discover that he was of Jewish origin. Saudi Arabia does not allow people of Jewish heritage to work in their country. It seems someone forgot an important prerequisite. The result was a huge expense, loss of lead-time, and loss of potential revenue.

But wait! The U.S. Equal Employment Opportunity Commission (EEOC) prohibits asking a person about his/her faith; so, even if someone had considered this possibility, there would have been a problem. Of course, there are creative ways of obtaining such information.

What is abundantly clear is that we should never engage in serious decision-making without:

- *Identifying all relevant criteria*
- *Segregating criteria and identifying obligatory criteria*
- *Assigning criteria weights to represent their significance*
- *Conducting a criteria sensitivity study (explained later)*
- *Identifying stakeholder expectations*

Selecting obligatory criteria, using a structured process allows us to defend our selection.

2.4 Candidate Selection

Candidates are the acceptable solutions to a problem — the options from which to implement. They are identified during the *problem-solving* phase.

Do not jump to conclusions thinking, "*My options are obvious.*"

Many experts who claim to have the answers have been proven wrong.

In 1899, the Commissioner of the US Patent Office recommended that the Patent Office be closed down because everything that could be invented had been invented and there was no longer any real need for such an office!

— *Creativity*

Irrespective of the decision-making tool you utilize, your best decision is only as good as your best candidate/option.

Thus, *creative thinking* is vital to generate a list of *good* candidates or options.

While most of us get trained in *critical thinking,* at some level, very few are exposed to the art of *creative thinking* – that which contributes to disruptive breakthroughs.

Caution! It is easy to reject an idea or a candidate, but it requires creative thinking and more energy to generate one in the beginning. Having a reasonable selection of candidates is highly desirable; but, as we learned, too many choices will make the decision-making process confusing and frustrating. So, be selective!

— *"Perishability"*

During candidate selection, it is important to ask the question:

> …. *are the candidates perishable*?

When we refer to perishable goods, we usually think about food; yet, there are many other perishable items.

- Consider airline seats. If not sold prior to take-off, they have no value; they perish.
- The same is true of restaurant chairs, cinema seats, and even your barber's chair.
- Delivery *capacity* of gas transportation systems is also perishable; hence, it is traded like airline seats.
- The same is true of telephone lines, electrical power lines, etc.

If not utilized, their value at a given moment is gone—in essence, they perish without generating any revenue. Thus, when we consider candidates (possible solutions to a problem), we need to be cognizant of their perishable nature when considering their viability for successful implementation.

2.5 Judgment Table (JT)

Gathering Candidate Information

Now we are ready to deal with the candidates/options with which to make the best decision.

Each candidate has favorable and unfavorable features with respect to each criterion. Since data and information pertaining to the various criteria can be voluminous, and unmanageable, we summarize all the pros and cons in a *judgment table*.

Even if you do not use the techniques presented in this book, I urge you to summarize the information in a *judgment table*.

Furthermore, it is imperative that you question the information being provided to you. Pay particular attention to the quality of the information. Too often people make wild guesses, which become *facts* as they move from person to person. Often, during the information-gathering stage, you will identify new criteria that need to be considered. These must be added to your original criteria list.

I caution you not to cut corners, especially if a sub-optimal decision is likely to have serious consequences. Always build a (judgment) table for the candidates and write down the pros and cons. It does not take long, but it will be of enormous help to you when comparing candidates (options).

— Interpreting the Judgment Table (JT)

When we interpret candidate data, we make judgment calls.

If one candidate's score is 10% less than another's, this 10% might be interpreted as *very significant* by one decision-maker, while another might consider it to be *insignificant*.

In baseball, a batting average of 0.300 (30%) is considered excellent! Yet in basketball, a player who achieves less than 80% in free throws is considered very poor!

Here too, we inject our own values, preferences, and beliefs.

Typical Judgment Table

	Sydney	Singapore	Kuala Lumpur	Beijing	New Delhi
Language Barriers	None (English speaking)	English speaking; though each ethnic community has its own language	Some difficulty; State matters will be an issue	Serious; need translators, though professionals speak English	English is the second language. Most schools teach English
Safety	Very Good	Excellent	Unpredictable	Unpredictable	Good
Manpower Costs	Expensive	Very expensive	Reasonable for a big city	Reasonable for a big city	Reasonable for a big city
Real Est. Costs	Very high; outskirts are affordable	Prohibitively expensive	Very high; outskirts are affordable	Very high	Very high; outskirts are affordable
Pollution	Minimal; clean city with good health regulations	Minimal	Not serious; but hygiene is an issue	Highly polluted city	Some pollution; but hygiene is a bigger problem
Corruption	Not an issue	Officially not an issue; but might need some greasing	A moderate amount of corruption exists	Very prevalent, though the govt. has an official no-nonsense policy	Rampant
Utilities	Affordable and stable	Expensive, but stable	Very reasonable and stable	Very reasonable and stable	Good, but unstable
Taxation	Normal	High	Reasonable	Very high for foreign businesses	Very high for foreign businesses

Unfortunately, we cannot remove the decision-maker from the process. He is the decision-maker; and will insist that this is his decision. His biases and subjective behavior are unavoidable but manageable.

If we are comparing the prices of new cars, and the prices range from $25,000 to $32,000, normally we would consider such differences as significant. However, if you are a very rich individual, such differences are not that significant.

In such a situation, consider them as being of equal significance, in your evaluation. You may even consider removing this criterion from the evaluation altogether, as it might skew the evaluation.

PART III: 3

AHP and the XpertUS Software

What got you here, won't get you there!
Marshall Goldsmith - "Coaching Guru"

3.1 The Analytic Hierarchy Process (AHP)

AHP - The Analytic Hierarchy Process was first applied to decision theory by Dr. Thomas Saaty (Univ. of Pittsburgh), in 1970. Since then AHP has gained worldwide acceptance. Even the US Dept. of Defense used AHP in the 2005 study of "Closure of Military Bases."

Watch this video (2 min.): www.xpertus.com/bkvideo_pw.mp4

The justification for using the AHP/pairwise technique is best illustrated by considering just one criterion.

Imagine you are seated in an airport lounge. The faces of two beautiful ladies appear on a TV screen. I ask you to distribute 100 points between these two, reflecting your concept of beauty. You might say, 40-60, 50-50, 70-30, and so on. This is your choice.

A few minutes later, the TV screen displays four (4) pictures of ladies. Once again, I ask you to distribute 100 points among the four ladies. You do this again; it probably took you a little longer.

A few minutes later, seven pictures (7) are displayed and again, you are asked to distribute 100 points among these ladies. Now you simply give up.

You would agree that as the number of candidates increased, it became increasingly more difficult to make a reliable judgment. This short mental exercise confirms that comparing a pair requires less effort than comparing a group, and it is certainly far more reliable and consistent.

AHP: The following is an extract from Wikipedia:

Though using the Analytic Hierarchy Process requires no specialized academic training, it is considered an important subject in many institutions of higher learning, including schools of engineering and graduate schools of business. It is a particularly important subject in the quality field, and is taught in many specialized courses including Six Sigma, Lean Six Sigma, and QFD.

Nearly a hundred Chinese universities offer courses in AHP, and many doctoral students choose AHP as the subject of their research and dissertations. Over 900 papers have been published on the subject in China, and there is at least one Chinese scholarly journal devoted exclusively to AHP.

The International Symposium on the Analytic Hierarchy Process (ISAHP) holds biennial meetings of academics and practitioners interested in the field. At its 2007 meeting in Valparaiso, Chile, over 90 papers were presented from 19 countries, including the U.S., Germany, Japan, Chile, Malaysia, and Nepal.

Topics covered ranged from Establishing Payment Standards for Surgical Specialists, to Strategic Technology Road-mapping, to Infrastructure Reconstruction in Devastated Countries.

— *The Significance of the Difference*

Here we had seven contestants. People attempt to consider all of them and assign some rank based on a scale, say 1-5, or 1-10. Such an approach is hopelessly flawed. To indicate the degree of preference or significance, rather than compare all of them together, you must deal with a pair at a time. When you compare two at a time, it is easy for you to say that you prefer A over B, to some degree (e.g. I like A very much; B is only marginally better than A; B is significantly better, etc.).

The classical AHP process relies on this pairwise comparison and requires you to indicate the degree of preference.

What is significant is *the difference*; not the absolute values.

In essence, the entire process boils down to two questions:

1. *Which One* (of the two, do you prefer)?

2. *How Much* (degree of preference, or superiority)?

There is ample evidence to prove that AHP is reliable and consistent!

Beware: Do not confuse AHP with the *process of elimination* that your optician uses.

Degree of Preference
1 = Equal
3 = Weak
5 = Moderate
7 = Strong
9 = Absolute
You may also use
intermediate values: 2,4,6,8

3.2 The XpertUS Software

While it is possible to perform the pairwise calculations using a spreadsheet, it is very time consuming and tedious.

The XpertUS software allows you to navigate through your feelings, expectations, biases, limitations, etc., to arrive at a well thought-out decision. XpertUS does not make the decision; you make the decision!

XpertUS is the vehicle that leads you through the process.

You are always in control. You simply tell XpertUS how you feel about criteria and candidates.

XpertUS can be used to extract *obligatory* criteria. For example, when building a house, it might be obligatory to remain within a given budget, yet it might be desirable to make the bedrooms smaller in order to add a study.

XpertUS is designed to handle both *quantitative* and *qualitative* criteria.

The cost of a car is *quantitative*, while the comfort of the ride is *qualitative*.

Features:

- Ranks criteria and candidates
- Allows the user to conduct decision validation studies
- Allows consolidation and peer evaluation (ideal for Group/Team decision-making)
- Is Reliable and Consistent!

The complete solution of AHP is based on Eigen matrices, and is not within the grasp of the average industry professional.

There are many programs in the market, which provide the complete AHP solution. XpertUS is just one of them.

You do not need the XpertUS software to conduct an AHP ranking. A spreadsheet solution can be created easily as well.

> Many large organizations that have placed their faith in AHP include:
>
> ✓ British Airways: To choose the entertainment system vendor for its entire fleet (1998)
> ✓ Turkish Government: To determine where to relocate the city of Adapazari, which was devastated by an earthquake (2001).
> ✓ Shell Oil: To choose the best type of platform to build, to drill for oil in the North Atlantic (1987)
> ✓ US Dept. of Defense: In the highly political and controversial "Military Base Closure Study" (1998)

3.3 AHP – The Manual Process

We will discuss "Criteria Weighting" and "Candidate Ranking" using a case study where an Engineering Contractor is seeking to recruit a "Business Development Manager." In the original study, twelve criteria were considered, along with four candidates (decision options). However, for simplicity, here we will consider six of the criteria.

Fig. 1: Obligatory Criteria
1. Availability
2. Leadership Potential
3. Salary Expectation
4. Self-Motivated
5. Team Player
6. Temperament

First, we assign weights to the *obligatory* criteria (see Fig. 2), using AHP, to represent their significance. We caution the reader against using a simple distribution of weights, as there is ample evidence that demonstrates the weaknesses of such an approach.

Fig. 2: Criteria Layout   1   2   3   4   5   6

		AV	LP	SE	SM	TP	TM
1. Availability	AV	1	7				
2. Lead'shp Potential	LP	1/7	1				
3. Salary Expectation	SE	----	----	1			
4. Self-Motivated	SM	----	----		1		
5. Team Player	TP	----	----	----	----	1	
6. Temperament	TM	----	----	----	----	----	1

Secondly, we lay out the criteria in rows and columns as shown in Fig. 2.

For convenience, here we use a two-letter abbreviation to represent each of the criteria.

Thirdly, we compare the criteria in pairs. We start with AV (Availability) and LP (Leadership).

We always ask two questions:

1. *Which one* (do you prefer, or is more significant)?

2. *How much* (the degree of preference, of one over the other)?

Fig. 3: Degree of Preference
1 = Equal
3 = Weak
5 = Moderate
7 = Strong
9 = Absolute
You may also use intermediate values: 2,4,6,8

If we have a *strong* preference for AV over LP, we will represent this as "7". However, if our preference is for LP, we will represent this as "1/7". (See the scale in Fig. 3)

In either case, the opposing mirror cell would have the reciprocal value. Also note that the diagonal cells will have a value of "1", since we are comparing an item to itself.

Fig. 4: Criteria Weighting		1	2	3	4	5	6		
		AV	LP	SE	SM	TP	TM	Eigen Value	Wt. %
1. Availability	AV	1	2	3	1/4	1/5	7	1.132	17.65
2. Leadership Potential	LP	½	1	1/3	1/3	2	1/5	0.530	8.27
3. Salary Expectation	SE	1/3	3	1	3	3	4	1.817	28.34
4. Self-Motivated	SM	4	3	1/3	1	1/3	1/4	0.833	12.99
5. Team Player	TP	5	½	1/3	3	1	1/2	1.038	16.19
6. Temperament	TM	1/7	5	1/4	4	2	1	1.061	16.55
							Total >>>	6.411	100.0

Fig. 4 shows the complete solution for criteria ranking.

The approximate Eigen value is obtained by multiplying all the values for a given item (row), and taking its nth the root. [n= no. of criteria]

For SM, the Eigen value: is:

$\{4 \times 3 \times 1/3 \times 1 \times 1/3 \times 1/4\} \wedge (1/6) = 0.833$ [$0.833/6.411 = 12.99$]

(Note we have 6 criteria)

— Candidate Ranking

Now we use the judgment table to conduct our candidate ranking. Note that this *judgment table* is built on the basis of information we have at this time and for a particular scenario. At a later stage, the environment might change, and we may have to deal with a different scenario, hence a new *judgment table*.

As before, we conduct an AHP comparison; but this time we compare the candidates in pairs, against each other, *considering one criterion at a time.* As an example, here we create the table for the *Salary Expectation* criterion [Fig. 5], as we did for criteria.

Fig. 5: Salary Exp.   1   2   3   4

Salary Exp.		JN	KY	MY	SU	Eigen	Rank
1. Jane	JN	1	7	5	1/3	1.848	30.95
2. Kathy	KY	1/7	1	1/5	1/7	0.253	4.23
3. Mary	MY	1/5	5	1	1/5	0.669	11.20
4. Sue	SU	3	7	5	1	3.201	53.61
Total >>>						6.232	100.00

Here we are only concerned how the candidates rate, with regard to this criterion. Once we complete the first criterion we conduct similar evaluations for all other criteria.

(To conserve space, we have not shown the candidate evaluations for the other criteria.)

Fig. 6 –Final Matrix

	Availa-bility	Lead'shp Potential	Salary Expec.	Self Motivation	Team Player	Temperament	Final Rank
Criteria Wts	0.177	0.083	0.283	0.130	0.162	0.166	---
Jane	5.93	41.67	30.95	9.63	56.38	21.58	27.22
Kathy	21.58	41.67	4.23	9.63	26.34	18.99	17.11
Sue	53.50	8.33	11.20	55.79	11.78	53.50	31.32
Mary	18.99	8.33	53.61	24.95	5.50	5.93	24.35
						Total >	100.00

We now gather the results from all the AHP evaluations and set up a matrix table (Fig. 6). To obtain the final ranking we multiply the points obtained by each candidate, with the corresponding criteria, and normalize the total.

Let's look at Jane = 27.22

= 5.93 x .177 + 41.67 x .083 + 30.95 x .283 + 9.63 x .130 + 56.38 x .162 + 21.58 x .166

But, we see that Sue (31.32%) is the desired candidate, using the manual AHP process.

Note that even though the manual technique is a good approximation, it does have several shortcomings, which will be apparent in the next Section: *Decision Validation*. Additionally, through this example, we demonstrated how to handle Steps 6 & 7 of the Seven-Step Decision-Making Process.

Caution! You might not be happy when you see the final ranking. Sometimes it is not what your intuition led you to initially.

3.4 Decision Validation

In the previous Section, we laid out the steps for using AHP (albeit the approximate manual technique) to arrive at the *optimum* decision. We ranked the candidates to reflect the values & beliefs of the decision-maker, considering all the factors in play.

Fig. 7: Criteria & Candidates

Criteria
- Language Barriers
- US Relationships
- Market Opps
- Real Estate costs
- Bureaucracy
- Taxation

Candidates
- Sydney
- Singapore
- Kuala Lumpur
- Beijing
- New Delhi

Note that this ranking is unique to this particular decision-maker. Another person might generate a different ranking, and this is to be expected.

Fig. 8: Candidate Ranking	
Sydney	26.30
Singapore	16.30
Kuala Lumpur	17.50
Beijing	16.70
New Delhi	23.20

Now that we know the interaction of criteria and candidates, it is imperative that we revisit the process to see if any of the constraints we imposed might have been overly stringent. We refer to this as the *N-1 Analysis*.

Branch Office Location Exercise

This is best explained with an example of an Engineering Services company considering opening a branch office in Asia. They identified criteria and the candidate cities (Fig. 7).

Then they conducted the AHP/XpertUS evaluation, to assign criteria weights, and rank the candidates (see Fig. 8). Here we see that *Sydney* is the preferred location.

Fig. 9A shows the ranking of candidates if we were to remove one criterion at a time; i.e. with 5 criteria at play.

> *This is a one-key operation when using the "What-If" (WIF) module of the XpertUS software.*

From Fig. 9A we can see that if we could manage the issue of *bureaucracy*, then *New Delhi* is the preferred candidate of choice.

In fact, this company decided to open the office in India, partnering with a renowned Indian conglomerate that is adept at managing bureaucratic issues.

> *Note: In this figure, the label under each band indicates the criterion that has been removed.*

Recruiting Exercise

To further reinforce the N-1 validation process, let us consider a human resources example. The initial AHP evaluation determines that *Sue* is the optimum candidate.

In the original evaluation, *"availability, within two weeks"* was considered to be a requirement.

Now, the N-1 analysis shows that if we are willing to wait a little longer for Jane, then she is the better choice. See Fig. 9B

Now the question for management – *Are we willing to wait for Jane?*

In summary, if we had not conducted the decision validation (N-1 Analysis) we would not have seen the hidden advantage of opting for *Jane* (or for *New Delhi*, in the previous example).

A decision validation exercise is mandatory, at all times.

Watch these videos for a complete explanation of the decision validation process using the XpertUS software:

AHP Example (2 min.): www.xpertus.com/bkvideo_ahp.mp4

CB Example (1 min.): www.xpertus.com/bkvideo_cb.mp4

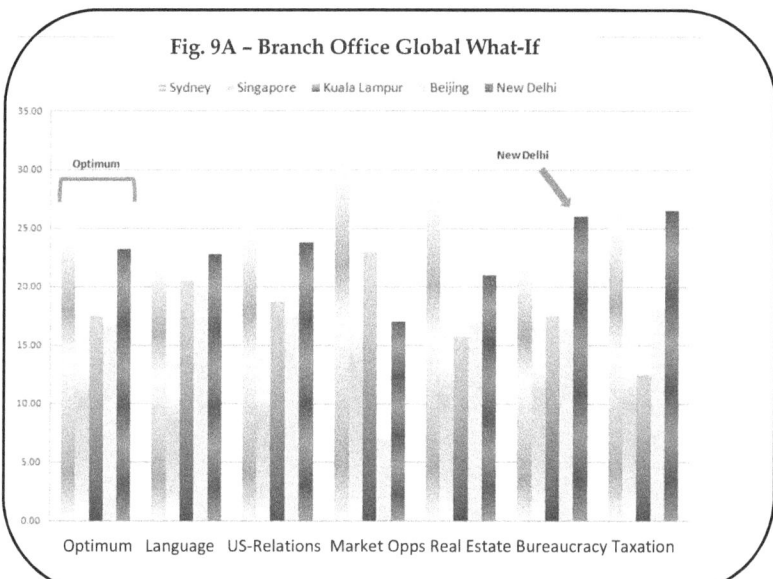

Fig. 9A – Branch Office Global What-If

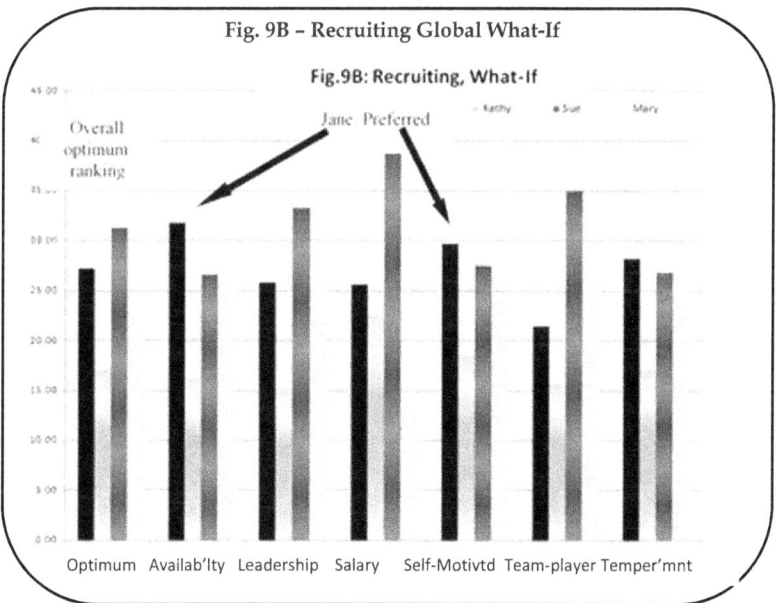

Fig. 9B – Recruiting Global What-If

Note: In this figure, the label under each band indicates the criterion that has been removed.

3.5 Cost-Benefit Analysis

The use of the AHP/XpertUS technique for cost-benefit analysis is best explained with an example – buying a laptop.

Step 1: Arrange the data/information about the laptops in the form of a judgment table. (See Fig. 10)

Fig. 10

	Criteria\Candidates	1 Dell Inspiron	2 HP ENVY	3 Lenovo 720S	4 Samsung	5 Acer
	Price	$899.00	$799.00	$999.00	$555.00	$666.00
1	Screen Size (inches)	13.3"	15.6"	13.3"	15.6"	13.3"
2	Proces. Speed (GHz)	1.8 Intel-i7	2.0 AMD E	1.8 Intel-i7	2.0 AMD E	1.8 Intel-i7
3	RAM (GB)	8 GB	16 GB	12 GB	8 GB	16 GB
4	Hard Drive (GB)	256 SSD	500 SATA	500 SSD	256 SSD	256 SSD
5	Avrg Batt Life (hrs)	12	8	10	8	8
6	Warrantee (months)	12	12	24	12	18
7	Construction	Good	Weak	V. Good	Weak	Good
8	Backlit Kbd	Yes	No	Yes	No	No

Step 2: Use XpertUS to assign criteria weights (Fig. 11)

Step 3: Use XpertUS for candidate evaluation (Fig. 12)

Fig 11: Criteria Wts (AHP)

Screen Size (inches)	9.070
Proces. Speed (GHz)	23.670
RAM (GB)	16.510
Hard Drive (GB)	18.110
Avrg Batt Life (hrs)	11.610
Warrantee (months)	11.020
Construction	4.500
Backlit Kbd	5.510
Total >>>>	100.000

Fig. 12: Example of Candidate Evaluation		
Screen (inch). - Weight	9.07	Rank
13.3"		65.00%
15.6"		35.00%
		100.00%

Enter the data from these two operations into the Excel sheet provided, and you will automatically see the cost-benefit graph (Fig. 13).

As you can see the ACER and the DELL offer similar benefits, but at vastly different costs.

This a powerful demonstration of the value of the pairwise technique in providing defensible decisions.

Important: Do not use "cost" in the above operations since the objective is to conduct a cost-benefit analysis.

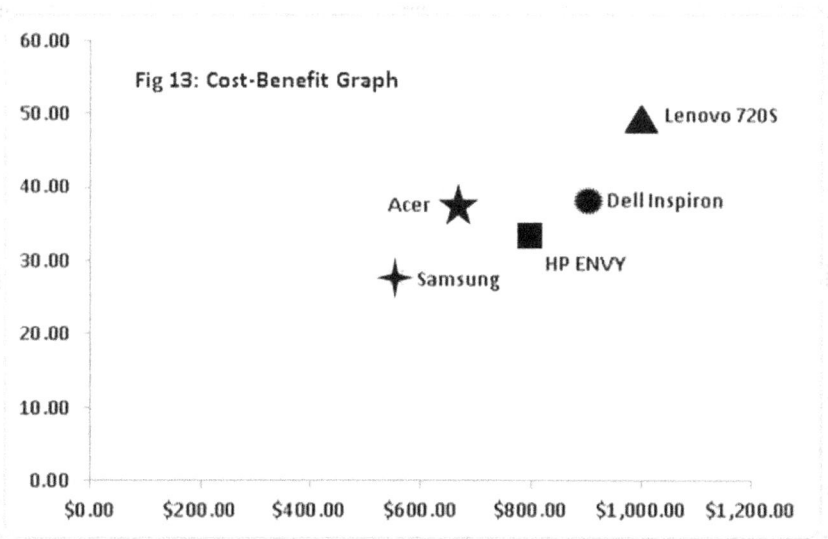

3.6 Team Decision-Making....

Working with Others

Whether it is the U.S. Congress or the Board of a large corporation, most crucial decisions are made within groups or teams. Some of the reasons for making decisions within teams are: *diverse viewpoints; specialized know-how/expertise; buy-in; uncertainty; consensus; anonymity; safety in numbers;* etc.

Often the group consists of representatives or specialists for each of the evaluation criteria. Where necessary, each specialist on the team may have his/her own sub-criteria.

— *Groupthink*

While groups can provide a range of specialized know-how, history has shown that groups are often ineffective at making optimum decisions.

Psychologist Irving Janis (Yale U.) called this phenomenon *Groupthink* – a deterioration of mental effectiveness, practical considerations, and moral judgment as a result of various group process factors.

Some may recall the disaster of the Challenger (January 28, 1986), a manned NASA space shuttle. Just over a minute into the flight, the shuttle exploded and burst into flames. The world was in shock. How could an eminent organization such as NASA have failed so catastrophically?

Following several high-level inquiries, a panel of experts concluded that the fundamental cause was an engineering flaw. The rocket seals had failed under freezing temperatures. Prior to the launch, engineers had reasons to believe there were potential seal problems. They had cautioned NASA against the launch until they had time to study this further. NASA made a bad decision. Were they victims of *Groupthink*?

A panel concluded that in the subsequent *Columbia* disaster, various committees had granted over 1600 safety waivers! *Groupthink*?

Harvey Pitt resigned (2003), after just 15 months in the job as Chairman of the Securities and Exchange Commission, among a myriad of allegations. Yet, earlier, the Senate had unanimously confirmed Pitt, hailing him as a savior. This is another example of the dangers of *Groupthink*.

Teams add a new dimension to our decision-making efforts. Nevertheless, the danger is that the team sees the problem through the same prism. Additionally, *people go along just to get along*. If you observe the dynamics of group interaction, you will observe the following:

1. *There will be a couple of natural leaders who are very vocal; they set the tone and direction of the discussion, with their own personal interests/objectives.*

2. *A few provide occasional input but are often forced into oblivion by the natural leaders.*

3. *Most try to maintain harmony or tend to stay in a comfort zone of no conflict. They contribute nothing to the event and basically go along with the crowd, eager to get back to things they are more comfortable with.*

It has been said that if Thomas Edison had worked with a focus group, he would have probably developed a very large candle, instead of the light bulb.

— *Disseminating; Storming; Refining; Deciding*

In an effort to diffuse *Groupthink*, before it can derail your team, we propose a modified approach to team meetings. Before you convene a meeting, establish the objective of the meeting, and let the participants know the purpose of the meeting. We suggest the following types of meetings:

1. *Disseminating* Meetings: The purpose of this meeting is to inform; very little interaction except for questions.

2. *Storming* Meetings: The objective is to look for creative solutions, seeking as many options as possible – QUANTITY!

3. *Refining* Meetings: These meetings are for discussion purposes; to present views, seek guidance, etc. – seeking QUALITY!

4. *Deciding* Meetings: Each team-member MUST make his/her own decision, prior to the meeting, and present it at the meeting. The team would then consider all the presentations and decide on a final acceptable decision, which might be a blend of several decisions.

— Consolidation Techniques

Consolidating individual decisions of several people is serious business; do not underestimate its significance. How the team consolidates the individual evaluations to arrive at the final ranking depends on the manner in which the individual evaluations are conducted. Let us consider the two main consolidation techniques.

A. Criteria-Consolidation

Each *group* leader is a member of the evaluation *team*. Here each *group* would conduct an independent evaluation, and rank the bidders considering only its specialty criterion. Typically one would use a comparative technique such as AHP/XpertUS.

The objective now is to consolidate the rankings obtained by the evaluators for the various criteria. Thus, we conduct a *criteria-consolidation*. This technique is perhaps best seen in terms of a project in which I was a consultant.

A Texas utility company invited bids from engineering companies to build and operate three pump stations. On this occasion we formed four groups of specialists, each representing a criterion, evaluating the bids for its specialty.

1. Group leaders assigned weights to the criteria, which represented the company philosophy. This is a critical step and we used AHP/XpertUS to minimize subjectivity.

2. Each group then used AHP/XpertUS and ranked the bids (candidates), considering only the sub-criteria for its specialty criterion.

3. Finally, we used a weighted average technique to obtain the final ranking of candidates.

If you do not have access to the XpertUS software, use your best judgment or the matrix method, for the final consolidation.

B. Decision-Consolidation

Examples of this type of decision-making would be a Board meeting, an Olympic figure-skating event, Recruiting, etc.

Each judge would submit his independent ranking of candidates, considering all criteria, using XpertUS or another technique. Thus we need to consolidate their decisions. We refer to this process as *decision-consolidation*, where all members have equal levels of authority.

The *decision-consolidation* technique is not suitable for evaluations of bids that have specialized criteria.

Consider the pump station example where teams were assembled with specialists from technical, operational, safety and financial areas. The *decision-consolidation* method would require people from the *financial* group to pass a value judgment on *technical* issues, and people from *safety* to render an opinion on *operational* issues. This is counter-productive to the evaluation.

In summary, real-world decisions are multi-dimensional:

1. *multiple criteria;*
2. *multiple candidates; and*
3. *multiple decision-makers.*

PART IV: 4

Decision Trees & D-Zone Maps

As we saw earlier, when we make decisions, we have to deal with criteria, which are the factors that drive our decisions.

However, often we have to deal with problems that are one-dimensional in nature, where the only criterion might be the *price*. In the case of a politician, the only criterion of significance might be *votes*. Uncertainty (probability) is inherent in these types of problems.

The Decision-Tree technique (DT) along with Decision-Zone Maps (DZ), are undoubtedly the best ways to deal with single-criterion problems, with uncertainties.

Caution: When dealing with probabilities we must consider two things:

The "event" probability (the likelihood of an event happening), and the "impact" probability (how it would affect us).

But first a word about DT basics. When drawing a DT, we use three (3) types of nodes:

- *Decision* nodes: where you have two or more options, and you have to make a decision (you have control).
- *Probability* nodes: where there is a probability of two or more events happening (you *do not* have control).
- *Terminal* nodes (endpoint): which represent an outcome.

The lines connecting these nodes to one another are referred to as *paths*. All paths must start and end with a node.

Probabilities

When you leave your home, to get to work, there might be a 30% chance (probability) you may run into heavy traffic. But, you also know that by leaving early, you may be able to reduce the probability of running into heavy traffic to 10%. Similarly, if you throw a die, you have a 1/6 (16.7%) chance of getting any one number.

As you can see, there is some degree of uncertainty in anything we consider. We can use this know-how to better estimate our chances of a satisfactory outcome.

If you plan on using the DT, you must understand the problem you are dealing with – so that you can break it down to its components. Additionally, you must be willing to deal with *probabilities*.

The best way to explain the DT is through an example.

Example: Bank Loan to Cement Factory (2 Options)

A cement factory is forced to default on a $20M bank loan. The Bank takes over the company and appoints a consultant to seek a solution. The consultant presents the following options:

Option 1: Inject $8M to upgrade the factory.

The success of such an initiative is estimated at 65% (successful turnaround). If successful, all debts would be paid in full; plus an additional "at risk" bonus of $5M. Otherwise, the only option is bankruptcy, with salvage value (See below).

Option 2: Do not invest

The consequences of such a decision would be:

- There is a 40% probability, the Government would nationalize the company (no payment) to ensure employment in the town. The probability of a turnaround is estimated at 10%. If successful they would pay back the $20M loan. No success, no liability.

- There is also a 30% likelihood that a competitor might acquire the company for $5M, to try to turn it around. The probability of a successful turnaround is estimated at 80%. If successful they would pay the balance $15M, plus a bonus of $15M. However, in the event its efforts are unsuccessful, they would not be liable for the balance of the loan.

- If neither of the above materializes, the company would be forced into bankruptcy and a salvage sale. Salvage recovery is estimated at $8M (35%) or $4M (65%).

What should the bank do?

Ignore time value, tax considerations, and the opportunity cost of money.

The next step is to build the DT in Excel watching these videos:

www.xpertus.com/bkvideo_bz.mp4

www.xpertus.com/bkvideo_jj.mp4

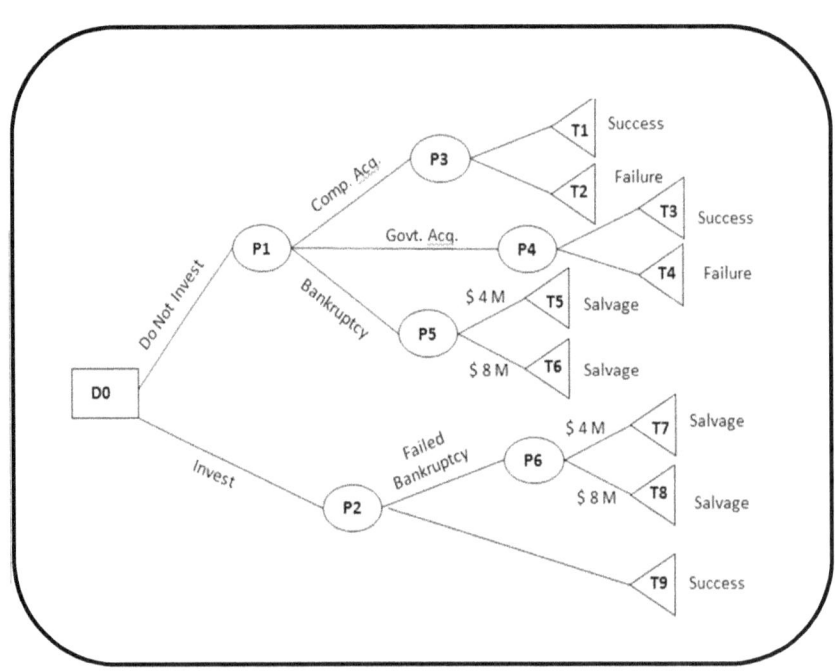

PART V: 5

The PayOff Table

When dealing with uncertainties, managing risk can be a daunting. Rather than make wild guesses, use a "payoff-table" to navigate through these uncertainties.

Example: On-Site Manpower (OSM)

On-Site Manpower supplies temporary labor to a construction site. Each morning OSM transports workers to a job-site that would hire up to 60 workers each day, based on the weather conditions on the day (rainy, mild, or sunny).

OSM has three vehicles that can transport 20, 40, and 60 passengers, and the transport costs are: $80, $110, and $145 respectively.

The wages per day: If hired = $20.00; if not hired = $11.00

OSM charges the job-site $37.00/day, per worker.

The historical hiring pattern during the last 150 days is as follows:

For 75 days (of the 150), they hired 18 workers; for 30 days, they hired 38 workers, and, for the balance 45 days, they hired 57.

How many should OSM plan on transporting each day (20, 40, or 60)?

In the payoff table the "*states of nature*" are the unpredictable scenarios of "rainy", "mild", and "sunny" days.

The correct approach would be to utilize *Decision Criteria*. Economists have identified these to be:

1. *MaxiMax*: Best of all "best" payoffs/outcomes.

2. *MaxiMin*: Least harmful of worst outcomes. We seek the "best" of the worst payoffs.
3. *Equally Likely* (Laplace): All "states" are equally likely to occur.
4. *Hurwicz* (Realism) Alpha: This is a compromise between the best and the worst.
5. *MiniMax Regret*: Regrets if not using the maximum payoffs (opportunity loss).
6. *Expected Value* (EV): With assumed probabilities.

The *states of nature* are the unpredictable scenarios of rainy, mild, and sunny days as shown in this table.

States of Nature >>	Rainy (18)	Mild (38)	Sunny (57)
Prob. >>>	0.5	0.2	0.3
20/day	204	260	260
40/day	-46	514	570
60/day	-301	259	791

Profit & Loss can be calculated using a simple Excel table. Enter the data as shown in the Excel PayOff Table, to obtain the best option for each decision criterion.

Transp. per day	Vehicle Cost	Demand per day	Hired per day	Not Hired per day	Profit	Loss	Net
20	$80.00	18	18	2	$306	$22	$204
40	$110.00	18	18	22	$306	$242	-$46
60	$145.00	18	18	42	$306	$462	-$301
20	$80.00	38	20	0	$340	$0	$260
40	$110.00	38	38	2	$646	$22	$514
60	$145.00	38	38	22	$646	$242	$259
20	$80.00	57	20	0	$340	$0	$260
40	$110.00	57	40	0	$680	$0	$570
60	$145.00	57	57	3	$969	$33	$791

Watch this 3-min. video for a complete explanation:

www.xpertus.com/bkvideo_po.mp4

APPENDIX I:

Understanding Risk: VUCA

The risks businesses face can be described with the acronym VUCA: *(Volatility, Complexity, Uncertainty, Ambiguity)*

In a *volatile* environment, we might know quite a bit about the situation, and we might be able to predict the outcome of our actions. The issue is simply the rapid rate of change. Most of us are in volatile markets with rapidly changing circumstances. Here is a typical example of a volatile environment in the restaurant industry.

> McDonald's rely on Anchovies from Peru as a supplement for cow-feed. Weather phenomena such as "El Nino" create volatility in the price they pay for Anchovies.

In *uncertain* situations, we might know quite a bit about the situation, but unsure how next to proceed. This is closely aligned with the military term "the fog of war."

> E.g. As governments change, taxation policies change. There is a lot of uncertainty, which impacts the stock markets, and interest rates.

Complexity represents a situation where we may be aware of the outcome of our actions, but we may have many key decision factors that are clouding our ability to make a defensible judgment.

E.g. the battle against ISIS was very complicated.

- The USA and Turkey demanded that Syrian President Bashar Al Assad is replaced.

- However, the Russians were supporting Assad, against the wishes of the USA and Turkey.
- Everyone needed the Kurds to move against ISIS on the ground. But Turkey is at war against the Kurds, who are seeking autonomy.
- Iran fought against ISIS, alongside the USA (Iran's arch enemy)
- Now Turkey and the USA are in a dispute over tariffs and hurling threats and insults at each other.

These types of problems are often referred to as *wicked problems*.

In the presence of *Ambiguity*, both the situational awareness and the predictability of the outcome of our actions are very low.

> E.g. A good example is when pioneering occurs on many levels at one time: new technologies, new ways of learning, new organizational structures and new business models. There are many moving parts, most of which have not been tried.

The distinctions between *volatile, uncertain, complex* and *ambiguous* business environments are not clear-cut.

Yes, it is important to customize your strategy to the situation, but don't worry too much about which aspect of VUCA you're dealing with.

VUCA is simultaneously a danger and an opportunity. While the environment is ripe for a breakdown in organizations, it is equally fertile for breakthrough opportunities. ***VUCA*** is here to stay; and will be more relevant in the future.

APPENDIX II:

Famous Bad Decisions

1. M&M and ET

In 1981, Amblin Productions called the Mars Company and offered a simple cross-promotional opportunity:

"How about if we use M&Ms in our new Steven Spielberg film, giving you free publicity, and in return, you can promote our film in your packaging?" The advertising and marketing folks at Mars said "No."

The film was E.T. (the Extra-Terrestrial), and the rest is history.

Reese's Pieces (not-nearly-as-well-known as M&M), saw sales jump 65% in the months after the film was released featuring their product. But who could have predicted that "E.T." would become one of the most popular movies of all time?

(Umm..., Spielberg had only made "Jaws" five years earlier.)

2. Kodak and the Digital Camera

Founded in 1880, Kodak commanded 90 percent of the film market by the late 1970s, and 85 percent of the camera market.

In 1975, one of its engineers successfully built the world's first digital camera; a clunky box that could produce a 100,000-pixel image, the equivalent of 0.01 megapixels. Kodak instantly recognized the potential of the device to revolutionize photography and invested billions in its development.

But conservative forces within the company stalled the release of a digital camera, afraid to abandon the film-and-paper product line that had brought it untold riches. By the time Kodak finally shifted to digital in the late 1990s, the megapixel revolution had long passed it by.

In 2012, Kodak filed for bankruptcy protection, after laying off more than 50,000 employees.

3. Blockbuster Video passes on Netflix

In the late 1990s, an Internet upstart named Netflix began offering a DVD-by-mail service. The subscription service exploded in popularity.

In 2000, Netflix executives made an offer to Blockbuster CEO John Antioco. For $50 million, Netflix would join forces with Blockbuster and help it launch its own online and DVD-by-mail service. Antioco laughed Netflix out of the office, seeing it as a niche player.

Who's laughing now?

As of May 2017, Netflix was valued at more than $60 billion and Blockbuster — which filed for bankruptcy in 2010 — closed 90% of its retail stores and canceled its copycat DVD-by-mail service in 2013. The last store was closed in 2018.

Why would anyone have thought that moviegoers would abandon video rental stores for the convenience of online streaming?

(Well, because it makes complete sense.)

4. Excite passes on Google

Imagine a world without Google. It's difficult to picture, but it was almost the case when Google was still just a young company, incubating in Silicon Valley. It turns out that Excite (which has since evolved into Ask.com), had the chance to purchase Google when it was still very small, for a meager price of only $750,000. Excite balked at the opportunity, and the rest is history.

5. New Coke

Coke spent millions of dollars developing their *New Coke*.

On April 23, 1985, American consumers popped open their first cans of *New Coke*. Within days, hundreds of letters and phone calls poured into Coke's Atlanta headquarters demanding a return to the old formula. People began hoarding cases of old Coke and selling them on the black market. Apparently, throughout its meticulous product testing, Coke failed to ask the real question:

> *Do Coke drinkers even want a new Coke?*

On July 11, less than three months after its debut, *New Coke* was pulled from the shelves and replaced with Coca-Cola Classic (now simply called Coca-Cola).

6. Decca Studios & Beatles

In 1962, the Beatles auditioned at the London office of Decca Records. The executive in charge of talent rejected them: he thought they sounded too much like a currently popular group called "The Shadows". He told Beatles manager, Brian Epstein, "We don't like your boys' sound. Groups are out; four-piece groups with guitars, in particular, are finished."

Fact: over 2 billion Beatles albums have since sold worldwide.

7. Western Union and Bell

In 1876, Western Union had a monopoly on the most advanced communications technology available, *the telegraph*.

They were offered the patent on a new invention, *the telephone*.

William Orten (President) considered the whole idea ridiculous, and wrote directly to Alexander Graham Bell, saying, "After careful consideration of your invention, while it is a very interesting novelty, we have come to the conclusion that it has no commercial possibilities. What use could this company make of an electrical toy?"

Two years later, after the telephone began to take off, Orten realized the magnitude of his mistake and spent years (unsuccessfully) challenging Bell's patents.

8. Ross Perot and Microsoft

Can you imagine Microsoft under the tutelage of someone other than Bill Gates? In 1979, billionaire (and one-time presidential candidate) Ross Perot met with a 23-year old Gates, to purchase Microsoft. Perot found the $50M price-tag to be too high. Instead of negotiating, Perot passed on the opportunity; and Microsoft went on to change the modern world as we know it.

9. Ross Perot and Home Depot (HD)

The founders of Home Depot wanted an investment of $2M in exchange for 50% of HD. During the discussions, Perot told them that his associates did not drive Cadillac cars (which the founders were driving), and dressed in white shirts (one was wearing a blue shirt), and did not have facial hair (one had a mustache). The founders did not appreciate a partner who was so petty-minded, and the deal fell through. Based on the present valuation of HD, Perot had said goodbye to about $100B.

10. Yahoo

In 2008, Yahoo rejected an unsolicited $44.6B bid from Microsoft. In 2017, Yahoo (now OATH) was acquired by Verizon for about $4.5B.

11. Ford Motor Co. and the Minivan

When Ford Motor Company rejected Chief Engineer Harold Sperlich's idea of the minivan they probably lost out on one of the greatest opportunities in the history of the auto industry. Sperlich then teamed up with Lee Iacocca at Chrysler, who went on to produce the first minivan.

Today 50% of all household vehicles are either minivans or SUVs. Ford said the opportunity loss was in excess of $1B.

Some final thoughts.....

These are a few of the better known "terrible" decisions; there are countless more – too many to mention here.

Of course, it's easy to see the folly of these decisions in retrospect; hindsight is 20/20, and no one can make the *right* decision all the time. But if these unfortunate executives had approached their decisions with a little more curiosity, a little more open-mindedness, recognizing their own fallibility & limitations, and the perils of the VUCA world, they might have seen the other side of the deal.

Quite often, bad decisions result from invalid assumptions based on ego, wishful thinking, or fear, and lack of faith in their own advisors.

APPENDIX III:

Answers to Problems

Exercise 1A: Perception [From P. 27]

Rotate the image 90⁰ (counter-clockwise) and you will see a horse.

Exercise 1B: Perception [From P. 27]

On close observation, you should see an old woman and a young girl in this picture.

(Hint: The young girl's chin is the old woman's nose)

Exercise 2: Oil Price Crisis [From P. 45]

The figure shows the value of the Euro, increasing against the US$ (US$ devaluing). The direct correlation between the value of the US$ and the price of oil is obvious.

If we pay the oil producers with *cheap* dollars, they are going to demand more dollars! *Note: Oil is traded in US$.*

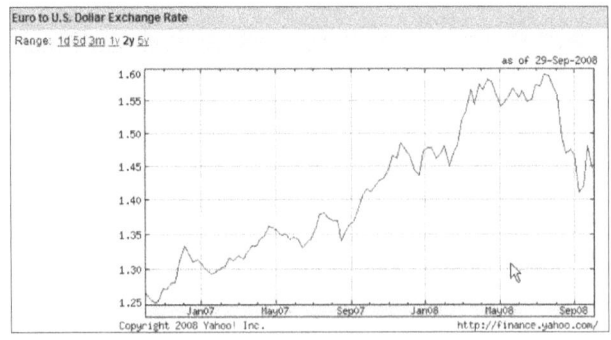

Q: Did you consider the "currency fluctuation" criterion?

ABOUT XPERTUS!

The XpertUS Decision Support System consists of:

1. Book: *Better Defensible Decisions*, by Dr. Errol Wirasinghe
2. Workshops: *Decision-Making: Perils & Remedies*
3. The XpertUS Multi-Dimensional Software
4. The XpertUS D-Zone Maps (MS Excel App.)
5. The Payoff Table (MS Excel App.)
6. Online Course on Decision-Making

All these are accessible from the website: www.XpertUS.com

No other individual/organization in the world can claim to have a complete suite of products that exclusively addresses this topic of decision-making.

Make the decision to get trained, and get your organization trained, as well.

Getting trained is like taking vitamins today, to avoid pain-killers tomorrow (damage control measures).

**All software products are issued free to those who attend our workshops, or take the online course!

Download the software from: www.xpertus.com/software.zip

www.ingramcontent.com/pod-product-compliance
Lightning Source LLC
Chambersburg PA
CBHW071056240526
45469CB00006BD/2317